THE *WILD BOY* *OF* *AVEYRON*

THE CENTURY PSYCHOLOGY SERIES

Richard M. Elliott, *Editor*

Kenneth MacCorquodale and Gardner Lindzey,
Assistant Editors

THE WILD BOY
OF AVEYRON

By

JEAN-MARC-GASPARD ITARD

Translated by

GEORGE & MURIEL HUMPHREY

With an Introduction by

GEORGE HUMPHREY

PRENTICE-HALL, INC., Englewood Cliffs, New Jersey

ISBN: 0-13-959494-9

Library of Congress Catalog Card Number: 62-16907

10 9 8 7 6

PRENTICE-HALL INTERNATIONAL, INC., *London*
PRENTICE-HALL OF AUSTRALIA, PTY. LTD., *Sydney*
PRENTICE-HALL OF CANADA, LTD., *Toronto*
PRENTICE-HALL OF INDIA PRIVATE LIMITED, *New Delhi*
PRENTICE-HALL OF JAPAN, INC., *Tokyo*

INTRODUCTION

The scene of the very human story described in this remarkable little book was laid in Paris at the end of the eighteenth and the beginning of the nineteenth centuries. Voltaire, the libertarian enthusiast, Montesquieu, master political analyst, Rousseau, clockmaker's son and fanatic of freedom, had all died within the generation just passing. The thought of these three great men had been transformed into action, or so it seemed, by the "savage dreamers" of the Revolution. A new era had begun. Medieval superstition was visibly dissolving at the touch of science. Had not one daring adventurer a few years before flown into the air in a fire balloon, while another crossed the straits of Dover in a similar contrivance? Had not Franklin "brought down the thunder from the clouds"? Had not Lavoisier finally swept away the pretensions of the alchemists and found a new science by splitting up water into two gases? Still more revolutionary to all previous conceptions was that remarkable new force, electricity, which Galvani and Volta had lately discovered. To the temper of the times it seemed that nothing was impossible to science. Man himself might be transformed. Reason alone was necessary to bring him, the noblest of all creatures, to the perfection that was his birthright. For the first time deaf-mutes might be taught to speak, and the blind to overcome their disability; Dr. Pinel had shown that even those unfortunate creatures, the insane, should be treated as curable patients, not as inmates of a human menagerie. It was a time of hope and enthusiasm for change. Even the years were no longer to be reckoned by the old method, but from the beginning of the new period of the revolution, and the months were to be known by rational names.

In these stirring times there lived at Paris a young medical man, Jean-Marc-Gaspard Itard, born in the provinces, who had early achieved some distinction in his profession and at the age of twenty-five was appointed physician to the new institution for deaf-mutes. A reflective, philosophically minded young practitioner, believing with the generous enthusiasm of youth in his own judgment, the future of his art, and the progress of humanity; willing, unlike many generous enthusiasts, to devote his time and thought to the improvement of mankind, and also, it must be said, to the business of proving himself right. A young man, Itard had the great advantage of not knowing too much. He could leap lightheartedly at a task before which maturity would quail. He had his opportunity.

In 1799, the year seven by the new calendar, there was published in the *Journal des Débats* a letter by one Citizen Bonaterre, describing a wild boy taken in the woods of the Department of Aveyron. According to reports, the child was a specimen of primitive humanity. He had been found almost unclad, wandering about at the outskirts of the forest in which he had apparently lived for some years, a stranger to human kind, eking out a precarious existence as best he could. The boy was brought to Paris and soon became a nine days' wonder. People of all classes thronged to see him, expecting to find, as Rousseau had told them, a pattern of man as he was: "when wild in woods the noble savage ran." What they did see was a degraded being, human only in shape; a dirty, scared, inarticulate creature who trotted and grunted like the beasts of the fields, ate with apparent pleasure the most filthy refuse, was apparently incapable of attention or even of elementary perceptions such as heat or cold, and spent his time apathetically rocking himself backwards and forwards like the animals at the zoo. A "man-animal," whose only concern was to eat, sleep, and escape the unwelcome attentions of sight-seers. Expert opinion was as usual somewhat derisive of popular attitude and expectations. The great Pinel examined the boy, declaring that his wildness was a fake and that he was an incurable idiot. In one of his standard works, indeed, this authority later speaks of "the pretended Wild Boy of Aveyron."

Among those who saw the child was the young Itard, who, fired with the notion that science, particularly medical science, was all-powerful, and perhaps believing that his older colleague was too conservative in applying his own principle of the curability of mental disease, came to the conclusion that the boy's condition was curable. The apparent subnormality Itard attributed to the fact that the child had lacked that intercourse with other human beings and that general experience which is an essential part of the training of a normal civilized person. This diagnosis Itard was prepared to back by an attempt at treatment, and the boy was consequently placed under the young doctor's care at the institution over which he presided.

By an unfortunate trick of fate Pinel's report is not available today. It was made before one of the learned societies which were beginning to be founded at the time, the name of which is not, however, recorded. Diligent search has failed to unearth the report.[1] Thus there is lacking today a most important source of firsthand information on the state of the boy when he was found. However, Itard has recorded what he heard at the meeting and, as far as it is possible to tell, has done so faithfully. Pinel's diagnosis was certainly uncompromising. As to the possibilities for the boy's future develop-

---

[1] Such search was made by the editor of the reprinted edition of Itard's reports; the present writer also searched in the libraries of Paris without result. Apart from Itard's own account there are available singularly few contemporary records of this popular sensation of the years 1799 and 1800.

ment he seems to have expressed a certain "philosophic doubt" consistent with what is to be expected of a master of the medical art, who "sees in the science of prognosis nothing but a more or less uncertain calculation of probabilities and conjectures." In the enthusiasm of youth, Itard was apparently equally uncompromising, but less philosophically doubtful. A certain knowledge of such writers as Locke and Condillac, often quoted, at least in Locke's case quite improperly, in support of the dictum: "Sense provides all," convinced him that he had only to find and apply the proper social and physical education in order to supply the mental content that would make of the boy a normal human being. It is certain that Itard was not so well acquainted with the work of these philosophers as in his youthful dogmatism he imagined. It is probable too that he was really misled by the little knowledge he had. Not only experience is necessary to make a normal human being, but also a mind capable of using experience. Nearly twenty years before, Kant had supplied this correction, but Itard had either not read Kant or had not realized the bearing of his work on the project in hand. At least he seems to have argued: "Here is a subnormal boy who has lacked civilizing experience. If I give him this experience he will become normal." The account of his five years' patient and ingenious endeavor to make good this deficiency is to be found in his two reports to the Minister of the Interior, now completely translated for the first time in spite of their recognized importance to psychology and the science of education. It is, of course, quite natural that revolutionary times should tend to regard human inequalities as due solely to human differences of education and experience.

It should be remembered in reading Itard's account that the boy in question was one of a number of such "wild" children found in the course of the sixteenth, seventeenth, and eighteenth centuries. In his *System of Nature,* published in 1735,

Linnaeus classifies the Wild Man (*Homo ferus*) as a distinct human species, describing him as "four-footed, mute, and hairy," [2] and mentions ten instances of varying dates from 1544 to 1731. Of these, eight are listed as girls, the rest as boys. Itard himself mentions one of them, a girl found in 1731 near Châlons-sur-Marne, but is inclined, probably with justification, to assign little scientific importance to the case. An account of this girl was published at the time, but the book is apparently not extant, nor is a copy of the translation to be found in the British Museum Catalogue. Another of Linnaeus' cases is mentioned in Birch's *History of the Royal Society* (1756). Under the date February 3, 1663, Birch gives the following note:

> Mons. Vossius communicated a relation of a child taken in Lithuania among bears in a bear-hunting, and then at the court of the Queen of Poland, where endeavours were used to reduce the child to some humanity, whence it seems to have altogether degenerated by long conversation with the wild beasts. This relation was attested by a French gentleman as an eye witness, . . . Sir Robert Moray was desired to make further inquiry into the fact by a letter to Dr. Davison, living in those parts. [3]

This case is listed by Linnaeus as *Juvenis ursinus lithuanus,* the bear-boy of Lithuania. Of the other cases reported by Linnaeus, apparently no trace can be found. These instances of "wildness" were well known at the time when Itard's boy was discovered, and he complains that the precious information they might have given had been lost owing to the defective state of science. Thus it was an old problem to which Itard was determined to apply the resources of the new science. Later research has uncovered a number of other cases. Of these the most comprehensive account known to the writer

---

[2] *Tetrapus, mutus, hirsutus,* as contrasted with *Homo sapiens,* who is described as *Homo diurnus, varians cultura loco.*

[3] Communicated by Mr. Harcourt Brown.

will be found in *Wolf Children and Feral Man* by J. A. L. Singh and Robert M. Zingg (Harper, 1942), now difficult to obtain. It is, however, indispensable for psychologists, sociologists, and others who wish to study the effects of different environments on very young children. Many of the earlier descriptions are, to say the least, semi-anecdotal and probably colored by what Freud calls "secondary elaboration," put in to improve the story. Nevertheless the book contains an important collection of "natural history" accounts. There may also be mentioned the late Professor Gesell's popular book, *Wolf Child and Human Child* (1941), a somewhat romantic account of an Indian "Wolf Girl" in which "narrative and comment are closely combined." This child was one of those trained by the Rev. and Mrs. Singh.

The question of the boy's mentality now arises. Following Pinel, it has generally been assumed that he was feeble-minded (his mental age has been estimated at about six years on this assumption). It has been seen that Itard disagreed with this diagnosis, though he probably changed his mind during the course of training. Certainly his efforts were not crowned with that triumphant success for which he had hoped, and which his first two years' experimentation led him to expect. Séguin claimed that the later methods of instruction were fitted rather to an idiot than to a savage. In a later paper [4] Itard speaks of the necessity for caution in diagnosis, adding, "it is because I have been deceived once that I make this observation." It is probable that he had the Wild Boy in mind. Today, 160 years after the event, it would seem rash to dispute the considered opinion of these two able eyewitnesses; yet a case has been made out for the boy's normality. [5]

---

[4] *Memoire sur le Mutisme produit par la lesion des fonctions intellectuelles* (reprinted with the original of the present translation, Paris, 1894), p. 113.

[5] Kellogg, W. N., "Humanizing the Ape," *Psychological Review* (1931), 38, 160.

It must be remembered that in practice it is hardly possible to find experimentally, according to the more rigorous standards of today, the exact effect of lack of human intercourse during the early, impressionable years, when the ordinary child is learning to be a human being. One form of experiment would need a number of pairs of identical twins, one reared in "ordinary," one in a highly impoverished environment such as the Wild Boy's. Such pairs are, to say the least, not easy to find! A further difficulty arises when it is remembered that the most famous of multiple births, the Dionne Quintuplets, said to be "more alike than the two sides of your face" showed considerable differences in, e.g., age of talking, and general character. There have, of course, been many cases where the degree of difference from standard environment is less than that of the Wild Boy. Identical twins have been reared apart, having been separated early in life. Speaking generally, the greater the environmental difference the greater the twin difference, though twins, again in general, did not differ as much over-all as ordinary brothers and sisters. *Personality factors seemed in these studies to be most susceptible to environmental influence, physical least, intelligence between them.* (H. H. Newman, F. N. Freeman, and K. J. Holzinger, *Twins; a study of heredity and environment* (Chicago, University of Chicago Press, 1937). McNemar, Psych. Bull., 35 (1938). Hilgard has an excellent summary in *Introduction to Psychology,* 2nd ed. (New York, Harcourt, Brace & World, 1958), p. 459.)

At ten years of age Itard's boy could not be taught to become a normal human person; logically it does not follow that he would have been unteachable at an earlier age. Of two of the "Wolf Children" of India, approximately two and eight years old respectively,[6] one was taught for four years, during which time she learned to say forty words. The vocab-

[6] Squires, P. C., "Wolf Children of India," *Amer. Journal of Psychology* (1927), 38, 313.

ulary of Itard's boy was much smaller. At the end of two years' training he could say *"lait"* and *"Oh Dieu"* and articulate a few comments. All later attempts to enlarge this speaking vocabulary were in vain. "I abandoned my pupil to an incurable dumbness," says his master. However, the child did acquire a very considerable reading vocabulary, learning, by means of printed phrases, to execute such simple commands as to pick up a key. It may be pointed out that, in contrast to the wolf child, Itard's boy had probably not even the advantage of hearing such patterns as the howling of the wolves in the cave. The wolf child learned to walk but not to run and in other respects was inferior to Itard's pupil. Thus the two children appear to have been comparable in mental development. Did it chance that in these two cases two originally feeble-minded children happened to undergo these incredible adventures? Or were either or both of them abandoned at an early age because they were feeble-minded? It is impossible to say. At least the suggestion that the boy described in these memoirs may originally have been of normal mentality is an interesting one. It has the weight of authority against it, and can unfortunately never be either proved or disproved.

Of the immediate success of Itard's work there is no question. In place of the hideous creature that was brought to Paris, there was to be seen after two years' instruction an "almost normal child who could not speak" but who lived like a human being; clean, affectionate, even able to read a few words and to understand much that was said to him. The news spread throughout Europe, and brought Itard a European reputation. Indeed the Emperor of Russia, through his ambassador, made him a flattering offer to settle in St. Petersburg, an invitation which, however, was refused after deliberation. As to the methods employed to obtain these results, they are admirably related in Itard's own clear language, and no attempt will be made in this introduction to anticipate the instructor's own account. It may nevertheless be said that for fertile ingenuity, tireless persistence, and that quick human sympathy which characterizes all great educators, the twenty-five year old doctor has hardly been excelled among teachers. Happy the child, normal or deficient, whom chance had brought to such a master! There are, however, certain general points where Itard's account is of peculiar interest to present-day psychology. To two of these, brief allusion will be made.

There has been much discussion in psychological and sociological literature as to the relative part played by heredity and environment in determing human nature.

Assuming that Pinel's diagnosis was the correct one, and that the boy was of subnormal mental capacity, there remains the fact that the child at first lacked certain very primitive activities which were afterwards taught him. It has already been mentioned that he apparently found difficulty in walking, preferring to trot. He could not climb onto a chair. He literally did not "know enough to come in out of the rain." Certain still more elementary modes of response were lacking. Thus his senses were extraordinarily apathetic. His nostrils were filled with snuff without making him sneeze. He picked up potatoes from boiling water. A pistol fired near him provoked hardly any response, though the sound of cracking a walnut caused him to turn round. These deficiences were all remedied by Itard's careful and ingenious treatment. Many mental defectives, as a matter of fact, show similar failings, which, upon careful treatment, prove curable by the use of methods similar to those which Itard devised. Indeed, the first great step in the education of the feeble-minded was taken by Edouard Séguin, Itard's pupil, who employed what he called the physiological method which has much in common with the procedures described by Itard, especially those in the latter part of the book. Before this time it had been believed that idiots [7] were ineducable—this in spite of Pinel's diagnosis and Itard's results. Séguin showed beyond all doubt that this view was mistaken, and his achievements gained him the title of the "Apostle of the Idiot."

Now the physical and mental structure of all human beings, feeble-minded and normal alike, develops through the interplay of hereditary and environmental conditions. After the fertilization of the ovum, every particle of matter in the human organism is contributed from the environment, the interaction of specific environmental conditions with a fertilized ovum of a definite character determining the nature of the resulting structure. Environmental influences begin before birth and continue after birth as general environment, both physiological and social; those environmental influences that are deliberately and systematically applied we call formal education. Itard's original mistake was apparently to assume, as the result of a somewhat amateurish philosophy, that environment could accomplish everything; that a boy who was not a normal human being could necessarily be made normal by the proper training. He failed to see that, even though he had been correct in this supposition, the environmental corrective must be applied at the right time. Training may clearly be too late—or too early.

On the other hand, most of the experts of the time went on the implicit supposition that in certain cases even properly organized environmental influence can have no effect. "It is useless to combat idiocy," said the *Dictionnaire de Médecine* nearly forty years later.[8] Itard's account is especially valuable because it clearly shows the error of both these extreme views.

---

[7] By "idiot" both here and in France was understood what is now termed "mentally deficient." It is of interest that the word originally had a social significance.

[8] Quoted by Boyd.

It abounds with instances of modes of behavior which, because of their primitive nature and their universality in normal human beings, have unthinkingly been taken to be due to "innate" factors, but which in common with all other human structures and modes of action, also require for their development the co-operation of the proper environmental conditions. The boy did not drop a hot potato. This was because his organism had not met with the special conditions in the environment that were necessary to develop or perhaps to fixate this action. Given such proper conditions in the form of Itard's training, the "normal" action developed, together with the underlying neural pattern. With the normal human being, all this happens so universally and the consequent "modification" of human structure and behavior takes place so naturally, that we are apt to forget that both environment and heredity have played a part. But, on the other hand, if the necessary initial hereditary conditions are not present, environmental conditions, however well organized, are powerless. Thus Itard was wrong in apparently assuming that training could give everything. This is not to say that he explicitly held such an absurd opinion as that anyone could be taught anything. The point undoubtedly never occurred to him, and it was obscured by this rather superficial reading of the empirical philosophers, Locke and Condillac.

The whole history of the education of the feeble-minded is thus pertinent to the old controversy between the "hereditarians" and the "environmentalists." With its brilliant initial success, its final uncovering of limitations, set off as they were against a background of environmentalist dogma on Itard's side and hereditarian dogma on the side of conservative opinion, this long educational experiment excellently illustrates the fundamental principles at issue.

Among the many other points of interest for the psychologist and the sociologist should also be mentioned the boy's reactions at the age of puberty. Consistently with modest experimental findings, we see the child clearly restless, under the sway of an urge, but not knowing how to gratify.

It would seem that the new uneasiness was in some vague way connected with the opposite sex, though it is difficult to see how this association could have come about. According to Freudian theory it may have come from very early memories, before he was abandoned. The activities connected with sex show again the close interrelation between the innate and the acquired, the learned and the non-learned, though on a different plane and this time in the sphere of social psychology. Physiologically, the sexual structures presuppose a social stimulus, one, that is, originating in another person of the same species. Sexual differentiation is due to an innate difference, present at the time of fertilization, but, like all such differences, it requires again the proper environmental conditions to bring it to fruition. These conditions involve both physiological and social environment. An important part of the latter is sexual education, which may again be conducted formally or informally, the latter method being almost universal in our civilization until the last generation or so. Here Itard's wild boy had not passed the proper conditions for structural development, but the social environmental factor had been lacking. With the possible exception of the organs of speech, and even these are said by some to act as functional integrations of pre-linguistic structures—the sexual activities give the only example of structural differences presupposing social stimulation in the human being. To contradict Aristotle, man is not physiologically a social animal save in the one respect of sex.

Finally, as to the historical place of Itard's work. Those who are specifically interested in this question are referred to William Boyd's excellent work, *From Locke to Montessori,*[9]

[9] Harrap, London, 1914.

containing a chapter which puts Itard in his proper setting. It may be said, however, that Itard was teacher of Séguin, already mentioned for his pioneer ways on the education of the feeble-minded. In his turn, Séguin deeply influenced Madame Montessori, who at the beginning of her career worked with feeble-minded children and obtained remarkable results by the use of his system. Later Séguin's devices were incorporated into the Montessori method of teaching normal children. Consequently the work of the young Paris doctor has ultimately influenced the education of many thousands of modern children through what has been perhaps the most widely known of all the speedy systems of education in the twentieth century. Many references to Itard's work are to be found in Dr. Montessori's books; not all of them, it may be said, are free from error.

Of the two memoirs here translated, the first was originally published in 1801 as a separate work, while the second was submitted by request in 1806 as a report to the Minister of the Interior. The style is singularly lucid and precise. Itard's writing has the clarity that comes of painstaking composition. We know that the expression of thought in literary form did not come easily to him. But although he is writing as a scientist, and is indeed rated by his eulogist Bousque as one of the greatest of medical stylists, the reader will find in these memoirs no dispassionate case-history. Throughout his five years' labors, Itard was intensely conscious of the pathos of his task, and of his responsibility in undertaking completely to change the world of another human being. "Unhappy creature," he cried after one particularly disappointing experience, "since my labors are wasted and your efforts fruitless, take again the road to your forest and the taste for your primitive life. Or if your new needs make you dependent upon a society in which you have no place to expiate your misfortune, die of misery and boredom at Bicêtre." "Scarcely had I finished," he adds, "when I saw his chest heave noisily, his eyes shut, and a stream of tears escape through his closed eyelids." Victor's pleasure in the sights of the country, Victor dining in town, Victor burning up his ninepins, such childish incidents are related with the touch of tenderness that can spring only from a deep human sympathy. At times, pathos is indeed strained almost to the point of breaking. Victor had been punished for stealing by such expedients as having his "pockets emptied of the little provisions which he had put in reserve an instant before." Such retaliation had the desired effect of stopping the pilfering. But Itard wished to find whether the boy regarded this treatment as an act of justice, or merely as one of vengeance. Consequently he took the course of doing the boy an obvious injustice. After a successful experiment, instead of the usual rewards the child was met with a severe and menacing expression." The praised work was angrily destroyed, books and cards were scattered in all directions and the child dragged towards a dark closet which had sometimes been used as a punishment. The boy resisted; Itard used force, when the child turned and violently bit the doctor's hand. He writes:

It would have been sweet to me at that moment could I have made my pupil understand and have told him how the pain of his bite filled my heart with satisfaction and made amends for all my labor. . . . It was an incontestable proof that the feeling of justice and injustice . . . was no longer foreign to the heart of my pupil.

It is difficult to read the passage with dry eyes.

From the literary point of view the second of the two memoirs is perhaps a little less carefully composed. It may be that Itard's growing reputation allowed him to be somewhat less painstaking. Perhaps the enthusiasm of youth was waning. Perhaps the growing sense of failure in his chief endeavor took away his zest for writing. In spite of five years' devoted and ingenious tutelage, the boy never became a normal human being.

The Wild Boy died, at about forty years of age, in 1828. Ten years later his kind-hearted preceptor, Itard, Member of the Academy of Medicine, passed away, leaving a high and still lasting reputation for his fundamental work on the education of the deaf-mute and on the diseases of the ear and, not least, for his stout-hearted and fruitful championship of the Savage of Aveyron.

GEORGE HUMPHREY

The present translation has been made from the reprinted edition of 1894 (*Rapports et Mémoires sur le Sauvage de L'Aveyron,* Paris) which is now out of print. The translators wish to thank Dr. Marcel Tirol, of the Department of French of Queens University, who generously read the manuscript and made many valuable suggestions. They wish to acknowledge also the very valuable literary and other assistance of Professor and Mrs. Elliott and the valuable legal assistance of Mr. Eric Scorer who cleared up some legal complications occurring between the two editions.

CONTENTS

FOREWORD BY THE AUTHOR

CAST upon this globe without physical strength or innate ideas, incapable in himself of obeying the fundamental laws of his nature which call him to the supreme place in the universe, it is only in the heart of society that man can attain the preëminent position which is his natural destiny. Without the aid of civilization he would be one of the feeblest and least intelligent of animals—a statement which has been many times repeated, it is true, but which has never yet been strictly proved. The philosophers who first made this statement, those who later upheld and taught it, have pointed to the physical and mental state of certain wandering tribes, which they regard as uncivilized because they are not civilized in our particular manner, and from which they have deduced the primitive characteristics of man as he exists in the pure state of nature. No, in spite of all assertions to the contrary, this is not the place to seek and study Man. In the most vagrant and barbarous horde as well as in the most civilized nation of Europe, man is only what he is made. Necessarily brought up by his own kind, he has acquired from them his habits and his needs; nor are his ideas any longer his own. He has enjoyed the fairest prerogative of his kind, the capacity of developing his understanding by the power of imitation and the influence of society.

The really wild type of man, one who owes nothing to his peers, ought then to be sought elsewhere. He ought to be reconstructed from the specific histories of a small number of individuals who, in the course of the seventeenth and beginning of the eighteenth centuries, have been found at different intervals living isolated in the woods, where they had been abandoned at a very early age.[1]

But in those unenlightened times so retarded was the progress of science—given up as it was to the mania for explanation, the uncertainty of hypothesis, and to investigation undertaken exclusively in the armchair—that actual observation counted for nothing and these valuable facts concerning the natural history of man were lost. The accounts left of them by contemporary authors are reduced to a few insignificant details, from which the most striking and most general conclusion to be drawn is that these individuals were susceptible to no very marked improvement. This was doubtless because the ordinary method of social instruction was applied to their education, without consideration for the difference of their organs. If the application of this method was entirely successful with the wild girl found in France towards the beginning of the last century, it is because, having lived in the woods with a companion, she already owed to that simple association a certain development of her intellectual faculties. This gave her a real education, such as Condillac [2] grants when he supposes two children abandoned in a profound solitude to whom the mere influence of cohabitation would naturally give scope for memory, imagination and even the invention of a few signs. This is an ingenious supposition fully justified by the story of the girl in question, in whom memory was found to be developed to the point where she could retrace in great detail some of the circumstances of her sojourn in the

[1] Linnæus has estimated these as ten in number and represents them as forming a variety of the human species. (*Système de la nature.*)

[2] *Essai Sur l'origine des Connaissances humaines,* 2nd part, first section.

woods and above all, the violent death of her companion.[3]

Deprived of these advantages the other children found in a state of individual isolation have brought to society only extremely sluggish powers. Their faculties were such that even if an attempt had been made to educate them, they would inevitably have defeated all the efforts of a metaphysics which was only just coming to life, and which was still hindered by the established doctrine of innate ideas. This metaphysics, united to a system of medicine fettered by entirely mechanical doctrines, could not rise to a philosophic treatment of the mind. Lighted by the torch of analysis and lending each other a mutual support, these two sciences have in our day laid aside their old errors and made immense progress. So it was reasonable to hope that if ever there appeared a creature similar to those of whom we have spoken, the sciences in question would bring to bear *all the resources of their present knowledge in order to develop him physically and morally,* or, at least, if this proved impossible or fruitless, there would be found in this age of observation someone who, *carefully collecting the history of so surprising a creature, would determine what he is and would deduce from what he lacks the hitherto uncalculated sum of knowledge and ideas which man owes to his education.*

[3] This girl was taken in 1731, in the vicinity of Châlons-sur-Marne, and brought up in a convent under the name of Mademoiselle Leblanc. When she could speak she told how she had lived in the woods with a companion, and how she had unfortunately killed her one day when they quarreled over the possession of a rosary which they had found under their feet. (Racine, *Poème de la Religion.*)

Although this story is one of the most circumstantial it is, nevertheless, so badly told that if what is insignificant and incredible is extracted there remain only very few particulars worthy of notice, the most remarkable of which is the faculty the young savage possessed of recalling her past state.

Dare I confess that I have proposed to myself both of these two great undertakings? But let no one ask me if I have reached my goal. This would be a very premature question which I could only answer at a time yet far distant. Nevertheless I might have waited in silence without wishing to trouble the public with an account of my labors, if it had not been a necessity as much as an obligation for me to prove, by my first successes, that the child with whom I have been concerned is not, as is generally believed, a hopeless imbecile but an interesting being, and one who merits from every point of view both the attention of observers and the particular care which is being devoted to him by the solicitude of an enlightened and philanthropic administration.

THE *WILD BOY*
OF *AVEYRON*

FIRST DEVELOPMENTS OF THE YOUNG
SAVAGE OF AVEYRON

A CHILD of eleven or twelve, who some years before had been seen completely naked in the Caune Woods seeking acorns and roots to eat, was met in the same place toward the end of September 1799 by three sportsmen who seized him as he was climbing into a tree to escape from their pursuit. Conducted to a neighboring hamlet and confided to the care of a widow, he broke loose at the end of a week and gained the mountains, where he wandered during the most rigorous winter weather, draped rather than covered with a tattered shirt. At night he retired to solitary places but during the day he approached the neighboring villages, where of his own accord he entered an inhabited house situated in the Canton of St. Sernin.

There he was retaken, watched and cared for during two or three days and transferred to the hospital of Saint-Afrique, then to Rodez, where he was kept for several months. During his sojourn in these different places he remained equally wild and shy, impatient and restless, continually seeking to escape. He furnished material for most interesting observations, which were collected by credible witnesses whose accounts I shall not fail to report in this essay where they can be displayed to the best advantage.[1] A minister of state with scientific interests believed that this event would throw some light upon the science of the mind. Orders were given that the child should be brought

[1] If the expression *Savage* has been understood until now to mean a man but slightly civilized, it will be agreed that this term has never been more truly merited. I will then keep to this name by which he has always been designated until I have given an account of the motives which determined me to give him another.

to Paris. He arrived there towards the end of September 1800 under the charge of a poor respectable old man who, obliged to part from the child shortly after, promised to come and take him again and act as a father to him should the Society ever abandon him.

The most brilliant and irrational expectations preceded the arrival of the Savage of Aveyron at Paris.[2] A number of inquisitive people looked forward with delight to witnessing the boy's astonishment at the sights of the capital. On the other hand many people otherwise commendable for their insight, forgetting that human organs are by so much less flexible, and imitation made by so much more difficult, in proportion as man is removed from society and from his infancy, believed that the education of this child would only be a question of some months, and that he would soon be able to give the most interesting information about his past life. In place of all this what do we see? A disgustingly dirty child affected with spasmodic movements and often convulsions who swayed back and forth ceaselessly like certain animals in the menagerie, who bit and scratched those who opposed him, who showed no sort of affection for those who attended him; and who was in short, indifferent to everything and attentive to nothing.

It can easily be understood that a creature of this kind could excite only a momentary curiosity. People ran in crowds, they saw him without observing him, they passed judgment on him without knowing him, and spoke no

[2] All that I have said and intend to say hereafter about the history of this child before his stay in Paris will be found to be guaranteed by the official reports of citizens Guiraud and Constant de Saint-Estève, government commissioners, the first near the canton of Saint-Afrique, the second near that of Saint-Sernin, and by the observations of citizens Bonaterre, professor of natural history in the Central School of the *Département de l'Aveyron* which are given in great detail in his *Notice historique sur le sauvage de l'Aveyron*.

more about him. In the midst of this general indifference the administrators of the National Institute of the Deaf and Dumb and its celebrated director never forgot that society, in taking over this unfortunate youth, had contracted towards him binding obligations that must be fulfilled. Sharing then the hopes which I founded upon a course of medical treatment, they decided that this child should be confided to my care.

But before the details and results of this decision are presented I must begin with an account of our starting point and recall and describe this first period, in order that the progress we have made may be better appreciated. By thus contrasting the past with the present, we can determine what ought to be expected from the future. Obliged then to return to facts already known, I will state these briefly; and that I may not be suspected of having exaggerated for the purpose of contrast, I will venture here to give a careful analysis of the description given of the boy, in a meeting to which I had the honor of being admitted, by a doctor whose genius for observation is as famous as his profound knowledge of mental diseases.

Proceeding first with an account of the sensory functions of the young savage, citizen Pinel showed that his senses were reduced to such a state of inertia that the unfortunate creature was, according to his report, quite inferior to some of our domestic animals. His eyes were unsteady, expressionless, wandering vaguely from one object to another without resting on anybody; they were so little experienced in other ways and so little trained by the sense of touch, that they never distinguished an object in relief from one in a picture. His organ of hearing was equally insensible to the loudest noises and to the most touching music. His voice was reduced to a state of complete muteness and only a uniform guttural sound escaped him. His sense of smell was so uncultivated that he was equally indifferent to the odor of perfumes and to the fetid exhalation of the dirt with which his bed was filled. Finally, the organ of touch was restricted to the mechanical function of the grasping of objects. Proceeding then to the state of the intellectual functions of this child, the author of the report presented him to us as being quite incapable of attention (except for the objects of his needs) and consequently of all those operations of the mind which attention involves. He was destitute of memory, of judgment, of aptitude for imitation, and was so limited in his ideas, even those relative to his immediate needs, that he had never yet succeeded in opening a door or climbing upon a chair to get the food that had been raised out of reach of his hand. In short, he was destitute of all means of communication and attached neither expression nor intention to his gestures or to the movements of his body. He passed rapidly and without any apparent motive from apathetic melancholy to the most immoderate peals of laughter. He was insensible to every kind of moral influence. His perception was nothing but a computation prompted by gluttony, his pleasure an agreeable sensation of the organ of taste and his intelligence the ability to produce a few incoherent ideas relative to his wants. In a word, his whole life was a completely animal existence.

Later, reporting several cases collected at Bicêtre of children incurably affected with idiocy, citizen Pinel established very strict parallels between the condition of these unfortunate creatures and that of the child now under consideration, and convincingly established a complete and perfect identity between these young idiots and the Savage of Aveyron. This identity led to the inevitable conclusion that, attacked by a malady hitherto regarded as incurable, he was not capable of any kind of sociability or instruction. This was the conclusion which citizen Pinel drew but which, nevertheless, he accompanied by that philosophic doubt which pervades all his writings, and which accompanies the predictions of the man who estimates the science of prognosis at its true worth, seeing in it nothing but a more or less uncertain calculation of probabilities and conjectures.

I never shared this unfavorable opinion and in spite of the truth of the picture and the justice of the parallels I dared to conceive certain hopes. I founded them for my part upon the double consideration of the cause and the curability of this apparent idiocy. I cannot go further without dwelling a moment upon these two considerations. Moreover, they bear upon the present and depend upon a series of facts which I must relate, and to which I shall see myself obliged more than once to add my own reflections.

If it were proposed to solve the following problem of metaphysics: *to determine what would be the degree of intelligence and the nature of the ideas of an adolescent, who, deprived from his childhood of all education, had lived entirely separated from individuals of his own species,* unless I am greatly mistaken the solution of the problem would be found as follows. There should first be assigned to that individual nothing but an intelligence relative to the small number of his needs and one which was deprived, by abstraction, of all the simple and complex ideas we receive by education, which combine in our mind in so many ways solely by means of our knowledge of signs, or reading. Well, the mental picture of this adolescent would be that of the Wild Boy of Aveyron and the solution of the problem would consist in exhibiting the extent and the cause of his intellectual state.

But in order to justify still further my opinion of the existence of this cause, it is necessary to prove that it has operated for a number of years, and to reply to the objection that can be made and that has already been made to me, that the so-called savage was merely a poor imbecile whom his parents in disgust had recently abandoned at the entrance to some woods. Those who lend themselves to such a supposition had not observed the child shortly after his arrival in Paris. They would have seen that all his habits bore the mark of a wandering and solitary life. He had an insurmountable aversion to society and to its customs, to our clothing, our furniture, to living in houses and to the preparation of our food. There was a profound indifference to the objects of our pleasures and of our fictitious needs; there was still in his present state, in spite of his new needs and dawning affections, so intense a passion for the freedom of the fields that during a short sojourn at Montmorency he would certainly have escaped into the forest had not the most rigid precautions been taken, and twice he did escape from the house of the Deaf and Dumb in spite of the supervision of his governess. His locomotion was extraordinary, literally heavy after he wore shoes, but always remarkable because of his difficulty in adjusting himself to our sober and measured gait, and because of his constant tendency to trot and to gallop. He had an obstinate habit of smelling at anything that was given to him, even the things which we consider void of smell; his mastication was equally astonishing, executed as it was solely by the sudden action of the incisors, which because of its similarity to that of certain rodents was a sufficient indication that our savage, like these animals, most commonly lived on vegetable products. I said most commonly, for it appeared by the following incident that in certain circumstances he had devoured small dead animals. A dead canary was given him and in an instant the bird was stripped of its feathers big and little, opened with his nail, sniffed at and thrown away.

Other indications of an entirely isolated, precarious and

wandering life are the nature and the number of scars with which the child's body is covered. To say nothing of the scar which is visible on his throat and which I shall mention elsewhere as having another origin and meriting particular attention, there could be counted four upon his face, six along his left arm, three at some distance from the right shoulder, four at the margin of the pubis, one upon the left buttock, three on one leg and two on the other which makes twenty-three [3] altogether. Of these some appeared to be due to bites of animals and the others to scratches which were more or less large and deep, forming numerous and in-effaceable evidences of the long and total abandonment of this unfortunate creature. When considered from a more general and philosophic point of view, these scars bear witness equally against the feebleness and insufficiency of man when left entirely to himself, and in favor of the resources of nature which, following apparently contradictory laws, work openly to repair and conserve that which she tends secretly to impair and to destroy.

Let us add to all these facts derived from observation those not less authentic to which the inhabitants of the country near the woods in which he was found have testified. We shall find that in the first days following his entrance into society, his only nourishment was acorns, potatoes and raw chestnuts, that he made no sort of sound, that in spite of the most active supervision he succeeded several times in escaping, that he showed a great repugnance to sleeping in a bed, etc. We shall find above all that he had been seen more than five years before entirely naked and fleeing at the approach of men,[4] which presupposes that he was already, at the time of his first appearance, habituated to this manner of life, which could only be the result of at least two

[3] Note. The figure 26 is given under the boy's portrait (tr.).
[4] Letter of citizen N——, inserted in the *Journal des Débats*.

years' sojourn in uninhabited places. Thus this child had lived in an absolute solitude from his seventh almost to his twelfth year, which is the age he may have been when he was taken in the Caune woods. It is then probable, and almost proved, that he had been abandoned at the age of four or five years, and that if, at this time, he already owed some ideas and some words to the beginning of an education, this would all have been effaced from his memory in consequence of his isolation.

This is what appeared to me to be the cause of his present state. It can be seen why I augured favorably from it for the success of my treatment. Indeed, considering the short time he was among people, the Wild Boy of Aveyron was much less an adolescent imbecile than a child of ten or twelve months, and a child who would have the disadvantage of anti-social habits, a stubborn inattention, organs lacking in flexibility and a sensibility accidentally dulled. From this last point of view his situation became a purely medical case, and one the treatment of which belonged to mental science, that sublime art created in England by Willis and Crichton, and newly spread in France by the success and writings of Professor Pinel.

Guided much less by the spirit of their doctrine than by their precepts, which could not be adapted to this unforeseen case, I classified under five principal aims the mental and moral education of the Wild Boy of Aveyron.

1st Aim. To interest him in social life by rendering it more pleasant to him than the one he was then leading, and above all more like the life which he had just left.

2nd Aim. To awaken his nervous sensibility by the most energetic stimulation, and occasionally by intense emotion.

3rd Aim. To extend the range of his ideas by giving him new needs and by increasing his social contacts.

4th Aim. To lead him to the use of speech by inducing

the exercise of imitation through the imperious law of necessity.

5th Aim. To make him exercise the simplest mental operations upon the objects of his physical needs over a period of time afterwards inducing the application of these mental processes to the objects of instruction.

I

First Aim. *To interest him in social life by rendering it more pleasant to him than the one he was then leading and above all more like the life which he had just left.*

This sudden change in his manner of life, the continued pestering of inquisitive people, a certain amount of ill-natured treatment which was the inevitable effect of living with children of his own age, seemed to have extinguished all hope of civilizing him. His petulant activity had insensibly degenerated into a dull apathy which had produced yet more solitary habits. Thus, except for the occasions when hunger took him to the kitchen, he was always to be found squatting in a corner of the garden or hidden in the attic behind some builders' rubbish. It was in this unfortunate condition that certain inquisitive persons from Paris saw him, and after an examination of some minutes judged him fit to be sent to an asylum; as if society had the right to tear a child away from a free and innocent life, and send him to die of boredom in an institution, there to expiate the misfortune of having disappointed public curiosity. I believed that there was a simpler and above all, a more humane method, namely, to treat him kindly and to exercise great consideration for his tastes and inclinations. Madame Guérin, to whom the authorities had confided the special care of this child, has performed and is still performing this exacting task with all the patience of a mother and the intelligence of an enlightened teacher. Far from opposing his habits, she has been able somehow to compromise with them and in that way to realize this first aim.

As far as one could judge of the past life of this child by his present inclinations, it was clear that, like certain savages from hot countries, his knowledge was limited to four things, viz. sleeping, eating, doing nothing and running about the fields. It was necessary then to make him happy in his own way, by putting him to bed at the close of day, supplying him abundantly with foods to his taste, respecting his indolence, and by accompanying him whenever possible for walks, or rather scampers, no matter what the weather was. These rural excursions seemed even more pleasing to him when a sudden or violent change in the weather occurred, so true it is that whatever condition he may be in, man is greedy for new sensations. Thus, for example, when watched inside his own room he was seen swaying with a tiresome monotony, turning his eyes constantly towards the window, looking sadly over the airy plains outside. If at such a time a stormy wind chanced to blow, if the sun behind the clouds showed itself suddenly illuminating the atmosphere more brightly, there were loud bursts of laughter, an almost convulsive joy, during which all his movements backwards and forwards very much resembled a kind of leap he would like to take, in order to break through the window and dash into the garden. Sometimes instead of these joyous movements there was a kind of frantic rage, he writhed his arms, pressed his closed fists upon his eyes, gnashed his teeth audibly and became dangerous to those who were near him.

One morning when there had been a heavy fall of snow while he was in bed, on awakening he uttered a cry of joy, left the bed, ran to the window, then to the door, going and coming with impatience from one to the other and finally escaped half dressed and gained the garden. There, giving vent to his delight by the most piercing cries, he ran, rolled himself in the snow and gathered it by handfuls, feasting on it with incredible eagerness.

But it was not always that his sensations would be expressed in such a lively and noisy manner at the sight of these grand effects of nature. It is worthy of notice that in certain cases they appeared to assume the stillness of regret and of melancholy—a very hazardous conjecture and one doubtless much opposed to the opinions of metaphysicians, but one which could not be gainsaid when this unfortunate youth was observed carefully and in certain circumstances. Thus, when the inclemency of the weather drove everybody from the garden, that was the moment when he chose to go there. He went round it several times and finished by sitting upon the edge of the pond.

I have often stopped for hours with inexpressible delight to consider him in this situation. I noticed how all these spasmodic movements and this continual swaying of his whole body diminished, subsiding by degrees and giving place to a more tranquil attitude. By what imperceptible stages his face, vacant or grimacing, took on a very decided expression of sadness or of melancholy reverie, as his eyes clung fixedly to the surface of the water, while from time to time he threw in some débris or dried leaves! During the night by the beautiful light of the moon, when the rays of this heavenly body penetrated into his room, he rarely failed to waken and place himself before the window. He stayed there, according to the report of his governess, for part of the night, standing motionless, his neck bent, his eyes fixed upon the moon-lit fields giving himself up to a sort of contemplative ecstasy, the silence and immobility of which were only interrupted at long intervals by deep inspirations nearly always accompanied by a plaintive little sound. It would have been as useless as inhuman to try to oppose these new habits and it even entered into my mind to associate them with his new existence in order to render it more agreeable. It was different with such habits as had the disadvantage of exercising his stomach and muscles continuously, thus leaving the sensibilities of the nerves and the faculties of the brain without action. Thus I made it my aim, and gradually succeeded in my attempt, to render his excursions less frequent, his meals fewer and less plentiful, his time in bed much shorter, and his days more profitable from the instructional point of view.

II

Second Aim. *To awaken his nervous sensibility by the most energetic stimulation, and sometimes by intense emotion.*

Certain modern physiologists have suspected that sensitiveness is directly proportional to civilization. I do not believe that a stronger proof of this could be given than the dullness of the Wild Boy of Aveyron's sense organs. The reader may convince himself by a glance at the description that I have already given which rests on facts drawn from the most authentic source. Relative to the same subject I will add here some of my most striking observations.

Several times during the course of the winter I have seen him crossing the garden of the Deaf and Dumb, squatting half naked upon the wet ground, remaining thus exposed for hours on end to a cold and wet wind. It was not only to cold but also to intense heat that the organ of the skin and touch showed no sensitivity. When he was near the fire and the glowing embers came rolling out of the hearth it was a daily occurrence for him to seize them with his fingers and replace them without any particular haste upon the flaming fire. He has been discovered more than once in the kitchen picking out in the same way potatoes which were cooking in boiling water, and I can guarantee that he had, even at that time, a fine and velvety skin.[5]

I have often succeeded in filling the exterior cavities of his nose with snuff without making him sneeze. The inference is that between the organ of smell, which was very highly developed in other respects, and those of respiration and sight, there did not exist any of those sympathetic relations which form an integral part of our sensibility, and which in this case would have caused sneezing or the secretion of tears. Still less was the secretion of tears connected with feelings of sadness, and in spite of innumerable annoyances, in spite of the bad treatment to which his new manner of life had exposed him during the first months, I have never discovered him weeping. Of all his senses, the ear appeared the least sensitive. It was found, nevertheless, that the sound of a cracking walnut or other favorite eatable never failed to make him turn round. This observation is quite accurate: yet, nevertheless, this same organ showed itself insensible to the loudest noises and the explosion of firearms. One day I fired two pistol shots near him, the first appeared to rouse him a little, the second did not make him even turn his head.

I have collated a number of similar cases where the lack of mental attention was taken for a lack of sensibility in the organ, but found, however, that this nervous sensibility was singularly weak in most of the other sense organs as well. Consequently it became part of my plan to develop it by all possible means, and to prepare the mind for atten-

[5] "I offered him," said an observer who had seen him at Saint-Sernin, "a great number of potatoes; he was delighted to see them, took them in his hands and threw them in the fire. He withdrew them an instant after and ate them burning hot."

tion by preparing the senses to receive keener impressions. Of the various means I employed, the effect of heat appeared to me best to fulfill this purpose. It is admitted by physiologists [6] and political theorists [7] that the inhabitants of the South owe their exquisite sensibility, so superior to that of the northerners, entirely to the action of heat upon the skin. I employed this stimulus in all possible ways. Not only was he clothed, put to bed, and housed warmly, but every day I gave him, and at a very high temperature, a bath lasting two or three hours during which frequent douches with the same water were administered to him on the head. I did not observe that the warmth and the frequency of the baths were followed by the debilitating effect attributed to them.

I should even have been glad if such had happened, convinced that in such a case the nervous sensibility would gain by the loss of muscular strength. But if the one effect did not follow, at least the other did not disappoint my expectations. After some time our young savage showed himself sensitive to the action of cold, made use of his hand to find out the temperature of the bath, and refused to enter when it was only lukewarm. For the same reason he soon began to appreciate the utility of clothes which until then he had only endured with much impatience. This utility once recognized, it was only a step to make him dress himself. This end was attained after some days by leaving him each morning exposed to the cold within reach of his clothes until he himself knew how to make use of them. A very similar expedient sufficed to give him at the same time habits of cleanliness and the certainty of passing the night in a cold wet bed accustomed him to get up in order to satisfy

[6] Lacose, *Idée de l'homme, physique et moral*—Laroche, *Analyse des fonctions du système nerveux*—Fouquet, article, "Sensibilité," de *Encyclopédie par ordre alphabétique.*

[7] Montesquieu, *Esprit des lois*, Book XIV.

his needs. To the administration of the baths I added the use of dry frictions along the spine and even ticklings of the lumbar region. This last means was more exciting than most. I even found myself obliged to reject it, when its effects were no longer limited to producing movements of pleasure but appeared to extend further to the generative organs and to add the threat of perversion to the first stirrings of an already precocious puberty.

To these various stimulants I had to add emotional stimulants which were no less exciting. Those to which he was susceptible at this time were confined to two, joy and anger. The latter I only provoked at long intervals, for its attack was most violent and always apparently justified. I remarked sometimes that in the force of his passion his intelligence seemed to acquire a sort of extension which furnished him with some ingenious expedient in order to get himself out of trouble. Once when we wanted to make him take a bath which was as yet only lukewarm and our reiterated entreaties had made him violently angry, seeing that his governess was not convinced of the coolness of the water by the frequent tests that he made with the tips of his own fingers, he turned towards her quickly, seized her hand and plunged it into the bath.

Let me relate another act of the same nature. One day when he was in my study sitting upon a sofa I came to sit at his side and placed between us a Leyden jar lightly charged. A slight shock which he had received from it the day before had made him familiar with its effect. Seeing the uneasiness which the approach of the instrument caused him I thought he would move it further away by taking hold of the handle. He took a more prudent course which was to put his hands in the opening of his waistcoat, and to draw back some inches so that his leg would no longer touch the covering of the bottle. I drew near him a second time and again replaced it between us. Another movement on his part, another adjustment on mine. This little maneuvre continued until, driven into a corner at the end of the sofa, he found himself bounded by the wall behind, by a table in front, and at my side by the troublesome machine. It was no longer possible for him to make any movement. It was then that, seizing the moment when I advanced my arm in order to guide his, he very adroitly lowered my wrist upon the knob of the bottle. I received the discharge.

But if sometimes in spite of the intense interest this young orphan inspired in me I took upon myself to excite his anger, I let no occasion pass of procuring happiness for him: and certainly this was neither difficult nor costly. A ray of sun reflected upon a mirror in his room and turning about on the ceiling, a glass of water let fall drop by drop from a certain height upon his finger tips while he was in the bath, and a wooden porringer containing a little milk placed at the end of his bath, which the oscillations of the water drifted, little by little, amid cries of delight, into his grasp, such simple means were nearly all that was necessary to divert and delight this child of nature almost to the point of ecstasy.

Such were, among a host of others, the stimulations, both physical and mental, with which I endeavored to develop the sensibilities of his organs. These methods produced after three months a general excitement of all the senses. His touch showed itself sensitive to the impression of hot or cold substances, smooth or rough, yielding or resistant. At that time I wore velvet breeches over which he seemed to take pleasure in passing his hand. It was with this exploratory organ that he nearly always assured himself of the degree to which his potatoes were cooked. Taking them from the pot with a spoon he would apply his fingers to them several times and decide according to their state of softness or resistance whether to eat them or throw them back again into the boiling water. When he was given a candle to light with some paper, he did not always wait until the fire had caught the wick before throwing the paper away hurriedly, although the flame was not yet near his fingers. If he was forced to push or to carry anything he would sometimes abandon it suddenly although it was neither hard nor heavy, in order to look at the ends of his fingers which were certainly neither bruised nor hurt, after which he would put his hand gently in the opening of his waistcoat. The sense of smell had also gained by this improvement. The least irritation of this organ provoked sneezing, and I judged by the fright that seized him the first time this happened, that this was a new experience to him. He immediately ran away and threw himself on his bed.

The refinement of the sense of taste was even more marked. The eating habits of this child shortly after he arrived at Paris were disgusting in the extreme. He dragged his food into the corners and kneaded it with his filthy hands.

But at the time of which I am now speaking it frequently happened that he would throw away in a temper all the contents of his plate if any foreign substance fell on it; and when he had broken his walnuts under his feet, he fastidiously wiped the nuts clean.

Finally disease itself, that irrefutable and troublesome witness of the characteristic sensitiveness of civilized man, came at this point to attest the development of this principle of life.[8] Towards the first days of spring, our young savage had a violent cold in the head and some weeks later two catarrhal affections, one almost immediately succeeding the other.

Nevertheless, all his organs did not respond so quickly. Those of sight and hearing did not participate in the improvement, doubtless because these two senses, much less

[8] I.e., Man's sensitiveness (tr.).

simple than the others, had need of a particular and longer education as may be seen by what follows.

The simultaneous improvement of the three senses, touch, taste and smell, resulting from the stimulants applied to the skin whilst these last two remained unaffected is a valuable fact, worthy of being drawn to the attention of physiologists. It seems to prove, what from other sources appears probable, that the senses of touch, smell and taste are only a modification of the organ of the skin; whereas those of hearing and sight, more subjective, enclosed in a most complicated physical apparatus, are subject to other laws and ought in some measure to form a separate class.

III

Third Aim. *To extend the range of his ideas by giving him new needs and by increasing his social contacts.*

If the progress of this child towards civilization and my success in developing his intelligence have hitherto been so slow and so difficult, I must attribute this more particularly to the innumerable obstacles I have met in accomplishing this third aim. I have successively shown him toys of all kinds; more than once I have tried for whole hours to teach him how to use them and I have seen with sorrow that, far from attracting his attention, these various objects always ended by making him so impatient that he came to the point of hiding them or destroying them when the occasion offered itself. Thus, one day when he was alone in his room he took upon himself to throw into the fire a game of ninepins with which we had pestered him and which had been shut up for a long time in a night commode, and he was found gaily warming himself before his bonfire.

However, I succeeded sometimes in interesting him in

amusements which had connection with his appetite for food. Here is one, for example, which I often arranged for him at the end of the meal when I took him to dine with me in town. I placed before him without any symmetrical order, and upside down, several little silver cups, under one of which was placed a chestnut. Quite sure of having attracted his attention, I raised them one after the other excepting that which covered the nut. After having thus shown him that they contained nothing, and having replaced them in the same order, I invited him by signs to seek in his turn. The first cup under which he searched was precisely the one under which I had hidden the little reward due to him. Thus far, there was only a feeble effort of memory. But I made the game insensibly more complicated. Thus after having by the same procedure hidden another chestnut, I changed the order of all the cups, slowly, however, so that in this general inversion he was able, although with difficulty, to follow with his eyes and with his attention the one which hid the precious object. I did more; I placed nuts under two or three of the cups and his attention, although divided between these three objects, still followed them none the less in their respective changes, and directed his first searches towards them. Moreover, I had a further aim in mind. This judgment was after all only a calculation of greediness. To render his attention in some measure less like an animal's, I took away from this amusement everything which had connection with his appetite, and put under the cups only such objects as could not be eaten. The result was almost as satisfactory and this exercise became no more than a simple game of cups, not without advantage in provoking attention, judgment, and steadiness in his gaze.

With the exception of amusements which like this lent themselves to his physical wants, it has not been possible for me to inspire in him a taste for those of his age. I am almost certain that if I could have done so I should have had great success. To appreciate this, one should remember the powerful influence exerted on the first development of thought by the games of childhood as well as by the little pleasures of the palate.

I have also done everything to awaken these last tendencies by means of the dainties most coveted by children and which I hoped to use as a new means of recompense, punishment, encouragement and instruction. But the aversion which he showed for all sweet substances and for our most delicate dishes was insurmountable. I then thought it advisable to try the use of seasoned dishes as being most suitable to arouse a sense necessarily dulled by rough foods. This was not any more successful and I offered him in vain, at such times when he was hungry and thirsty, strong liquors and spiced foods. Despairing at last of being able to inspire in him any new tastes, I cultivated the few to which he was limited by accompanying them with all accessories that could increase his pleasure in them.

It was with this intention that I often took him to dine with me in town. On such occasions there was on the table a complete collection of his favorite dishes. The first time that he found himself at such a feast there were transports of joy amounting almost to frenzy. Doubtless he thought that he would not do so well at supper time as he had just done at dinner, for on leaving the house that evening it was not his fault that he did not carry away with him a plate of lentils that he had pilfered from the kitchen. I congratulated myself on this first outcome. I had just procured him a pleasure; I had only to repeat it several times to make it a necessity. Which is what I actually did. I did more. I was careful to precede our expeditions by certain preparations which he would notice; these were to enter his home about four o'clock, my hat upon my head, his shirt folded in my hand. These preparations soon came to be for him the signal of departure. I scarcely appeared before I was understood; he dressed himself hurriedly and followed me with much evidence of satisfaction. I do not give this fact as proof of a superior intelligence and there is no one who will not object that the most ordinary dog will do at least as much. But in admitting this intellectual equality one is obliged to acknowledge a great change, and those who saw the Wild Boy of Aveyron at the time of his arrival in Paris, know that he was very inferior on the score of discernment to this most intelligent of our domestic animals.

It was impossible when I took him with me to go on foot. It would have been necessary for me to run with him or else to use most tiring violence in order to make him walk in step with me. We were obliged, then, to go out only in a carriage, another new pleasure that he connected more and more with his frequent excursions. In a short time these days ceased to be merely holidays to which he gave himself up with the liveliest pleasure, but were real necessities the privation of which, when there was too long an interval between them, made him sad, restless and capricious.

How the pleasure was increased when these parties took place in the country! I took him not long ago to the country house of citizen Lachabeaussière in the valley of Montmorency. It was a most curious sight, and I venture to say one of the most touching, to see the joy that was pictured in his eyes at the sight of the little hills and woods of that laughing valley. It seemed as if the eagerness of his gaze could not be satisfied through the windows of the carriage. He leaned now towards the one, now towards the other, and showed the liveliest anxiety when the horses went more slowly or were about to stop. He spent two days in this country house and such was the effect of these outside influences, of these woods, these hills, with which he could never satisfy his eyes, that he apeared more impatient and wild than ever, and, in the midst of the most assiduous and kind attention and most affectionate care, seemed to be occupied only with the desire to take flight. Entirely captivated by this dominant idea which absorbed all his faculties and even the consciousness of his needs, he scarcely found time to eat. He would get up from the table every minute and run to the window in order to escape into the park if it was open; or if it was shut, to contemplate, at least through the panes, all those objects towards which he was irresistibly attracted by still recent habits and perhaps even by the memory of an independent life, happy and regretted. I therefore resolved never again to submit him to similar tests. But in order not to sever him entirely from his country tastes, he was taken continually to walk in some neighboring gardens, of which the straight and regular arrangement had nothing in common with the great landscapes of which wild nature is composed, and which so strongly attach primitive man to the place of his childhood. Thus Madame Guérin took him sometimes to the Luxembourg and almost daily to the Observatory gardens where the kindness of citizen Lemeri has accustomed him to go every day for a lunch of milk. By means of these new habits, of certain recreations of his own choosing and finally, of all the kind treatment with which his new existence was surrounded, he finished by liking it all. This was the beginning of the intense affection which he has acquired for his governess and which he sometimes expresses in a most touching manner. He never leaves her without reluctance nor does he rejoin her without signs of satisfaction.

Once when he had escaped from her in the streets, he shed many tears on seeing her again. Some hours after, he still had a high and broken respiration and a kind of feverish pulse. When Madame Guérin reproached him, he interpreted her tone so well that <u>he began to weep</u>. The friendship which he had for me was much less strong, and justifiably so. The care which Madame Guérin takes of him is of a kind which is immediately appreciated, and what I give him is of no obvious use to him. That this difference is unquestionably due to the cause indicated is shown by the fact that there are times when he welcomes me and they are the times which I have never used for his instruction. For example, when I go to the house in the evening just after he has gone to bed, his first movement is to sit up for me to embrace him, then to draw me to him by seizing my arm and making me sit upon his bed, after which he usually takes my hand, carries it to his eyes, his forehead, the back of his head, and holds it with his upon these parts for a very long time. At other times he gets up with bursts of laughter and comes beside me to caress my knees in his own way which consists of feeling them, rubbing them firmly in all directions for some minutes, and then sometimes in laying his lips to them two or three times. People may say what they like, but I will confess that I lend myself without ceremony to all this childish play.

I shall perhaps be understood if my readers will remember the paramount influence exerted upon a child's mind by the inexhaustible delights and the maternal triflings that nature has put into the heart of a mother and which make the first smiles flower and bring to birth life's earliest joys.

IV

Fourth Aim. *To lead him to the use of speech by inducing the exercise of imitation through the imperious law of necessity.*

If I had wished to relate only happy results I should have suppressed from this account this fourth aim, the means I have employed in order to reach it and the slight success I have obtained in it. But my object is to give an account not so much of my own labors as of the first mental developments of the *Savage of Aveyron,* and I ought not to omit anything that can have the least bearing on this. I shall even be obliged to introduce certain theoretical ideas here and I hope that they will be pardoned when it is seen how careful I have been to found them on nothing but facts and when it is recognized that I was obliged to reply to the everlasting objections. *"Does the Savage speak? If he is not deaf why does he not speak?"*

It is easily conceived that in the midst of the forest and far from the society of all thinking beings, the sense of hearing of our savage did not experience any other impressions than those which a small number of noises made upon him, and particularly those which were connected with his physical needs. Under these circumstances his ear was not an organ for the appreciation of sounds, their articulations and their combinations; it was nothing but a simple means of self-preservation which warned of the approach of a dangerous animal or the fall of wild fruit. These are without doubt the functions to which his hearing was limited, judging by the slight response obtained from the organ given a year ago to all sounds and noises except those bearing upon his individual needs; and judging on the other hand, by the exquisite sensibility which this sense showed for such sounds as had some such connection with his interests. When a chestnut or a walnut was cracked without his knowledge and as gently as possible; if the key of the door which held him captive was merely touched, he never failed to turn quickly and run towards the place whence the sound came. If the organ of hearing did not show the same susceptibility for the sounds of the voice, even for the explosion of firearms, it was because he was necessarily little sensitive and little attentive to all other impressions than those to which he had been long and exclusively accustomed.[9]

It is understandable then why the ear, well qualified to perceive certain noises however slight, would not be apt to appreciate the articulation of sounds. Moreover in order to speak it is not sufficient to perceive the sound of the voice, it is necessary also to appreciate the articulation of that sound, two very distinct operations which require different conditions on the part of the organ. For the first a certain degree of sensibility of the auditory nerve is sufficient, for the second there must be a special modification of this same sensibility. It is possible then that certain well-organized and very quick ears may be unable to seize the articulation of words. Many mutes have been found among the Cretins

[9] In order to give more force to this assertion I shall observe that in proportion as man grows away from his childhood the exercise of his senses becomes less universal from day to day. During his earliest days he wishes to see everything and touch everything; he carries to his mouth everything that is given him; the least noise makes him tremble; his senses dwell on everything, even on those things which have no connection with his needs. In proportion as he leaves this epoch behind, which is in a way a sort of apprenticeship of the senses, objects make an impression on him only as much as they are related to his appetites, his habits or his inclinations. Even then it often happens that there are only one or two of his senses which awaken his attention. There is the expert muscian who, attentive to all he hears, is indifferent to all he sees. We have the technical mineralogist and botanist who in a fertile field when seeking material for their researches will see, the first only minerals, and the second nothing but vegetable productions. There may be a mathematician without ear who will whisper on leaving a play by Racine, "What does all this prove?" If then, after the early days of childhood, attention is given naturally only to such things which have recognized or suspected connection with our tastes, it is understood why our young savage, having only a small number of requirements, would exert them upon a small number of objects. Unless I am deceived, that is the cause of this absolute inattention which struck everybody at the time of his arrival at Paris, and which at the present moment has almost completely disappeared because he has been made to feel the connection which all the new things about him have with him.

who are nevertheless not deaf. Among the pupils of citizen
Sicard there are two or three children who hear perfectly the
sound of the clock, clapping of hands, the lowest tones of
the flute and violin, but who have however never been
able to imitate the pronunciation of a word even though it
may be articulated very loudly and slowly. Thus one might
say that speech is a species of music to which certain ears,
although perfectly constituted otherwise, may be insensible.
Will it be the same with the child here in question? I do
not think so, although my hopes have not much foundation.
It is true that my efforts here have not been very numerous
and that for a long time, uncertain as to the line I ought to
take, I restricted myself to the rôle of observer. This then
is what I have noticed. During the first four or five months
of his sojourn in Paris, the *Savage of Aveyron* only showed
himself sensitive to different noises which had for him the
association I have indicated. During the current November [10]
he has appeared to hear the human voice and when two
people conversed loudly in the corridor adjacent to his room
it occurred to him to go up to the door in order to reassure
himself that it was quite closed; he also closed an inside
swinging door, taking the precaution to put his finger on the
latch to secure its fastening still better. I noticed sometime
after that he distinguished the voice of the deaf and dumb, or
rather the gutteral cry which continually escapes them in
their games. He even seemed to recognize the place where
the sound came from, for if he heard it on coming down
the stairs he never failed to go up again or come down more
quickly according as whether the cry came from above or
below. At the beginning of December [11] I made a most
interesting observation. One day when he was in the kitchen

[10] Frimaire,—the third month of the calendar of the first French Re-
public, from 21st Nov. until 21st Dec. (tr.).

[11] Nivose,—the fourth month of the calendar .(tr.).

occupied with cooking potatoes two people had a sharp dispute behind him, without his appearing to pay the least attention. A third arrived unexpectedly, who, joining in the discussion, commenced all his replies with these words,— "Oh, that is different." I noticed that every time that this person let his favorite "Oh!" escape, the *Savage of Aveyron* quickly turned his head. That evening when he went to bed I made some experiments upon this sound and obtained almost the same results. I went over all the other simple sounds known as vowels but without any success. This preference for "O" obliged me to give him a name which terminated with this vowel. I chose Victor. This name remains his and when it is called he rarely fails to turn his head or to run up.

It is perhaps for the same reason that in the sequel he has understood the significance of the negative *Non* which I often used to correct him when he made mistakes in his little exercises.

In the middle of these slow but obvious developments of the organ of hearing his voice remained mute and refused to render those articulate sounds which his ear appeared to appreciate. However, the vocal organs in their exterior conformation presented no trace of imperfection and there was no reason for suspecting it in their interior organization. It is true that there is visible on his throat a very extended scar which might throw some doubt upon the soundness of the underlying parts if one were not reassured by the appearance of the scar. In fact it looks like a wound made by a sharp instrument but from its linear appearance one is inclined to believe that the wound was only a superficial one and that it would have reunited at the first attempt, or to use the technical term, by first intention. It is to be presumed that a hand with the will rather than the habit of crime had wished to make an attempt on the life of this child, and that, left for dead in the woods, he will have owed the prompt recovery of his wound to the help of nature alone. This recovery could not have been effected so happily if the muscular and cartilaginous parts of the organ of speech had been severed. Because of these considerations, when he did not repeat the sounds which his ear began to perceive, I did not conclude that this was due to an organic lesion, but merely to unfavorable circumstances. Complete absence of exercise renders our organs unfit for their functions; and if those already trained are so powerfully affected by this inaction, what will become of those which grow and develop without any incentive to put them into play? At least eighteen months of careful education are necessary before a child stammers a few words; and a rough inhabitant of the woods who has been in society for only fourteen or fifteen months, of which he has spent five or six among deaf mutes, is expected to be in a condition to talk! Not only is that impossible, but much more time and much more trouble will be necessary before coming to this important point in his education than would be needed for the least precocious of children. Such a child knows nothing, but he possesses in a marked degree the capacity of learning everything, an innate propensity to imitation, an extreme flexibility and sensibility of all organs, perpetual mobility of the tongue, an almost gelatinous consistency of the larynx. In short, every-thing coöperates to produce in him that continuous babbling which is the involuntary apprenticeship of the voice and which is assisted also by coughing, sneezing, the cries of that age, and even the tears, tears that must be considered not only as the indications of a ready excitability, but in addition as a powerful motive perpetually applied at the time most expedient for the simultaneous development of the organs of respiration, voice, and speech. Grant me these great advantages and I will guarantee the same result. Even admitting as I do that such a result can no longer be expected of the young adolescent Victor, it must also be realized that Nature is prolific enough to create new means of education when accidental causes intervene to deprive her of those that she had primitively arranged. Here are some facts at least which may justify this hope.

I said at the beginning of the fourth section that I proposed to lead him to the use of speech *by inducing the exercise of imitation through the imperious law of necessity.* By the considerations put forth in the last two paragraphs, and by another equally conclusive one which I will shortly set forth, I was convinced that a tardy functioning of the larynx must be expected and that I ought to accelerate its activity by coaxing it with something he wanted. I had reason to believe that the vowel "O," having been the first heard would be the first pronounced, and I found it very favorable to my plan that this simple pronunciation was, at least with respect to the sound, the sign of one of the most ordinary needs of the child. Nevertheless, I was unable to derive any advantage from this favorable coincidence. When his thirst was most intense, it was in vain that I held before him a glass of water, crying frequently *"eau" "eau."* [12] Then I gave the glass to someone else who pronounced the same word beside him, asking for it back in the same way. But the unfortunate creature, tormented on all sides, waved his arms about the glass almost convulsively, producing a kind of hiss but not articulating any sound. It would have been inhuman to insist further. I changed the subject without, however, changing the method. It was upon the word *lait* that I carried out my next experiments.

On the fourth day of this next experiment I succeeded to my heart's content, and I heard Victor pronounce distinctly, though rather uncouthly it is true, the word *lait,*

[12] "Water, Water," pronounced *o, o.* (tr.)

and he repeated it almost immediately. It was the first time that an articulate sound left his mouth and I did not hear it without the most intense satisfaction.

Nevertheless I made a reflection which in my eyes much diminished the advantage of this first success. It was not until the moment when, despairing of success, I came to pour the milk into the cup which he gave me, that the word *lait* escaped him with great demonstrations of pleasure; and it was only after I had poured it again as a reward that he pronounced it a second time. It can be seen why this result was far from fulfilling my intentions. The word pronounced instead of being the sign of his need was, relative to the time when it had been articulated, merely an exclamation of pleasure. If this word had been uttered before the thing which he desired had been granted, success was ours, the real use of speech was grasped by Victor, a point of communication established between him and me, and the most rapid progress would spring from this first triumph. Instead of all this, I had just obtained a mere expression, insignificant to him and useless to us, of the pleasure which he felt. Strictly speaking, it was certainly a vocal sign, the sign of possession. But this sign, I repeat, did not establish any relation between us. It had soon to be neglected because it was useless to the needs of the individual and was swamped by a multitude of irrelevancies, like the ephemeral and variable sentiment for which it had become the sign. The subsequent results of this misuse of the word have been such as I feared.

It was generally only during the enjoyment of the beverage that the word *lait* was heard. Sometimes he happened to pronounce it before and at other times a little after but always without purpose. I attach no more importance to this spontaneous repetition than to his repetition of it even now during the night when he happens to wake. Following this result I have entirely given up the method by which I obtained it. Awaiting the moment when circumstances will allow me to substitute another which I believe to be more efficacious, I have given over his vocal organs to the influence of imitation which, although feeble, is nevertheless not extinct, if judged by some slight subsequent and spontaneous progress.

The word *lait* has been for Victor the root of two other monysyllables *la* and *li*, to which he certainly attaches even less meaning. He has since modified the latter a little by adding a second *l* and pronouncing both like the *gli* in Italian. He is often heard to repeat *lli lli* with an inflection of voice not without sweetness. It is surprising that the liquid *l* which for children is one of the most difficult sounds to pronounce, should be one of the first that he has articulated. I am somewhat inclined to believe that in this painful linguistic labor there is a sort of feeling after the name of Julie, a young girl of eleven or twelve who comes to spend Sundays with Madame Guérin, her mother. Certain it is that on this particular day the exclamations *lli, lli,* become more frequent and, according to the account of his governess, are even heard during the night, at times when there is reason to believe that he is sleeping soundly. The cause and value of this last fact cannot be exactly determined. It is necessary to postpone its classification and description until a more advanced puberty has allowed us to make more observations. The latest accomplishment of his vocal organs is somewhat more considerable and is composed of two syllables which equal three because of the way he pronounces the last.

It is the exclamation *"Oh Dieu!"* which he has taken from Madame Guérin, and which he lets escape frequently in moments of great happiness. He pronounces it by leaving out the *u* in *Dieu,* and laying stress on the *i* as if it were double and in such a way as to be heard to cry distinctly, *Oh Diie! Oh Diie!* The *o* found in this last combination of sounds was not new to him; I had succeeded some time previously in making him pronounce it.

This is our present position with reference to the vocal organs. It is seen that all the vowels with the exception of the *u,* already enter into the small number of sounds which he articulates and that only three consonants are found *l, d,* and the liquid *l.* This progress is certainly very feeble if it is compared to that required for the complete development of the human voice; but it seems sufficient to guarantee the possibility of this development. I have already related the causes which would necessarily make this development long and difficult. There is still another which will have an equal effect in the same direction and which I ought not to pass over in silence. I allude to the facility with which our young savage expresses his few wants otherwise than by speech.[13] Each wish manifests itself by the most expressive signs which have in some measure, as have ours, their gradations and their equivalent values. If the time for his walk has come, he appears several times before the window and before the door of his room. If he then sees that his governess is not ready, he places before her all the objects necessary for her toilet and in his impatience even goes to help her dress. That done, he goes down first and himself pulls the check string of the door. Arriving at the Observatory, his first business is to demand some milk which he does by presenting a wooden porringer which, on going out, he never forgets to put in his pocket, and with which he first pro-

[13] My observations also confirmed the important opinion of Condillac upon this point who says in speaking of the origin of the language of sound, "The language of action, at that time so natural, was a great obstacle to surmount; could it be abandoned for another of which the advantages could not be foreseen, and the difficulty of which was so strongly felt?"

vided himself the day after he had broken in the same house a china cup which had been used for the same purpose.

Then again, in order to complete the pleasure of his evenings he has for some time past kindly been given rides in a wheelbarrow. Since then, as soon as the inclination arises, if nobody comes to satisfy it, he returns to the house, takes someone by the arm, leads him to the garden and puts in his hands the handles of the wheelbarrow, into which he then climbs. If this first invitation is resisted he leaves his seat, turns to the handles of the wheelbarrow, rolls it for some turns, and places himself in it again; imagining doubtless, that if his desires are not fulfilled after all this, it is not because they are not clearly expressed. Where meals are concerned his intentions are even less doubtful. He himself lays the cloth and gives Madame Guérin the dishes, so that she may go down to the kitchen and get the food. If he is in town dining with me, all his requests are addressed to the person who does the honors of the table; it is always to her that he turns to be served. If she pretends not to hear him, he puts his plate at the side of the particular dish which he wants and, as it were, devours with his eyes. If that produces no result, he takes a fork and strikes two or three blows with it on the brim of his plate. If she persists in further delay, then he knows no bounds; he plunges a spoon or even his hand into the dish and in the twinkling of an eye he empties it entirely in his plate. He is scarcely less expressive in his way of showing his emotions, above all impatience and boredom. A number of people visiting him out of curiosity know how, with more natural frankness than politeness, he dismisses them when, fatigued by the length of their visits, he offers to each of them, without mistake, cane, gloves and hat, pushes them gently towards the door, which he closes impetuously upon them.[14]

[14] It is worthy of notice that this language of action is entirely nat-

In order to complete the account of this pantomime language, I must also say that Victor understands it as easily as he uses it. If Madame Guérin wishes to send him to fetch some water it is enough for her to show him the pitcher and let him see it is empty by turning it upside down.

A similar procedure was enough to make him give me a drink when we dined together. But what is more astonishing in the way he lends himself to these means of communication is that he has no need of any preliminary lesson, nor of any mutual agreement in order to make himself understood. I convinced myself of this one day by a most conclusive experiment. I chose among a number of others, an object for which there existed between him and his governess no indicating sign, as I assured myself beforehand.

Such, for example, was the comb which was used upon him and which I wished to make him bring to me. When I appeared before him with my hair rough and bristling in all directions I should have been very much surprised if he had not understood me. He did indeed do so, and immediately I had in my hands what I wanted. Many people see in these proceedings only the behavior of an animal. For my part I will confess I believe that I recognize in them the language of the human species, originally employed in the infancy of society before the work of ages had coördinated the system of speech and furnished civilized man with a prolific and sublime means of improvement which causes his thought to blossom even in the cradle, and which he uses all his life

ural to him and that he used it in the most expressive manner from the first days of his entrance into society. "When he was thirsty," said citizen Constant-St. Estève, who saw him at the beginning of this interesting period, "he looked right and left; having noticed a pitcher he put my hand in his and led me towards it, striking it with his left hand in order to ask me for a drink. He was brought wine which he disdained, showing impatience at my delay in giving him water."

without appreciating what it is to him and what he would be without it if he found himself accidentally deprived of it, as in the case which now occupies us. Without doubt a day will come when the increased requirements of young Victor will make him feel the necessity of using new signs. The defective use which he made of his first sounds may delay this but not prevent it. It will perhaps be neither more nor less than what happens to the child who first lisps *papa,* without attaching to it any meaning and who from then on says it everywhere and on all occasions, gives it to every man he sees, and then, only after many reasonings and even abstractions, succeeds in giving it a simple and correct application.

V

Fifth Aim. *To induce him to employ the simplest mental operations over a period of time upon the objects of his physical needs, afterwards inducing the application of these mental processes to the objects of instruction.*

If we consider human intelligence at the period of earliest childhood man does not yet appear to rise above the level of the other animals. All his intellectual faculties are strictly confined to the narrow circle of his physical needs. It is upon himself alone that the operations of his mind are exercised. Education must then seize them and apply them to his instruction, that is to say to a new order of things which has no connection with his first needs. Such is the source of all knowledge, all mental progress, and the creations of the most sublime genius. Whatever degree of probability there may be in this idea, I only repeat it here as the point of departure on the path towards realization of this last aim.

I shall not enter here into details concerning the means employed to exercise the intellectual faculties of the *Savage of Aveyron* upon the objects of his appetites. These means were simply obstacles always increasing, always new, put between him and his wants, and which he could not overcome without continually exercising his attention, his memory, his judgment and all the functions of his senses.[15]

Thus all the faculties useful in his education were developed and it was only necessary to find the easiest way to turn them to account. I could no longer count upon much assistance from the sense of hearing, for in this respect the *Savage of Aveyron* was nothing but a deaf mute. This consideration forced me to try citizen Sicard's method of instruction. I began then with the procedure ordinarily used

[15] Here it is not amiss to remark that I have found no difficulty in accomplishing this aim. Wherever his wants were in question, his attention, his memory and his intelligence seemed to raise him above himself; this was always observable, and a due consideration of it would have led to the prediction of a happy future for him. I am not afraid to say that I regard as a great proof of intelligence the fact that after living for six weeks in human society, he had been able to learn to prepare his food with every care, the details of which citizen Bonaterre has passed on to us. "His occupation during his sojourn at Rodez," said this naturalist, "consisted in shelling kidney beans, and he fulfilled this task with that degree of discrimination employed by the most practised person. As if he knew by experience that these vegetables were intended for his maintenance, as soon as a vegetable basket was brought to him, he went for a pot and would establish the scene of the shelling in the middle of the apartment. There he distributed his materials in the most convenient way possible; the pot was placed to the right and the beans to the left; he opened the pods in turn, one after the other, with an inimitable suppleness of his fingers; he put the good beans in the pot and threw away again such as were musty or spotted. If by accident a bean escaped him, he followed it with his eyes, gathered it up and put it with the others. As he emptied the pods he placed them in an orderly pile at his side and when his work was finished, he lifted the pot, poured some water into it and carried it near to the fire, which he blazed up with the pods which he had piled up separately. If the fire was out, he took the shovel, put it in the hands of his guardian and made signs for him to go and look in the neighbourhood, etc."

first in that celebrated school and drew on a blackboard the
outline of some objects that could best be represented by a
simple drawing, such as a key, scissors, and a hammer.
Repeatedly, and at such times as I saw that I was being
noticed, I placed each of these objects upon its respective
drawing and when I was sure that in this way he had been
made to feel the connection, I endeavored to make him bring
them successively to me by pointing to the drawing of the
one I wanted. Nothing came of this. I repeated the experiment several times and always with as little success; he
either refused stubbornly to bring the one of the three
things which I indicated, or else brought the two others with
it and gave them all to me at the same time. I am convinced that this was merely calculated laziness which did
not let him do in detail what he found quite simple to do
all at once. I bethought myself then of a means which would
force him to give particular attention to each of these
objects. I had noticed for some months past that he had a
most decided taste for order; so much so that sometimes he
would get up from his bed to put a piece of furniture or a
utensil which had accidentally got moved, back again into
its usual place. He was even more particular about the
things hanging upon the wall: each had a nail and a particular hook, and when any of these had been changed he
was not quiet until he had himself corrected them. All I
had to do then was to arrange in the same way the things
upon which I wished him to exercise his attention. By means
of a nail I suspended each of the objects below its drawing
and left them there for some time. When afterwards I came
to give them to Victor they were immediately replaced in
their proper order. I repeated this several times and always
with the same result. Nevertheless, I was far from attribu-
ting this to his discrimination, and this classification could
well be only an act of memory. To reassure myself I changed

the respective positions of the drawings and this time I saw him follow the original order in the arrangement of the objects without any allowance for the transposition. As a matter of fact, nothing was easier than for him to learn the new classification necessitated by this change, but nothing more difficult than to make him reason it out. His memory alone bore the burden of each arrangement. I devoted myself then to the task of neutralizing in some way the assistance which he drew from it. I succeeded in fatiguing his memory by increasing the number of drawings and the frequency of their transpositions.

His memory now became an insufficient guide for the methodical arrangement of the numerous articles, so that one would expect his mind to find assistance by comparing the drawing with the things. What a difficult step I had overcome! I was convinced of this when I saw our young Victor fasten his gaze and successively, upon each object, choose one, and next look for the drawing to which he wished to bring it, and I soon had material proof by experimenting with the transposition of the drawings, which was followed on his part by the methodical transposition of the objects.

This result inspired in me the most brilliant hopes. I had believed there were no more difficulties to conquer, when there arose a most insuperable one which obstinately held me back and forced me to renounce my method. It is well known that in the education of the deaf and dumb this first procedure is followed by a second and much more difficult one. After having been made to feel by repeated comparisons the connection of the thing with its drawing, the letters which form the name of the object are placed on the drawing. That done, the drawing is effaced and only the alphabetical signs remain. The deaf mute sees in this second procedure only a change of drawing which continues to be for him the sign of the object. It was not so with Victor who, in spite of the most frequent repetitions, in spite of a prolonged presentation of the thing below its word, could never solve the problem. I was easily able to account for this difficulty and it was easy for me to understand why it was insurmountable. From the picture of an object to its alphabetical representation, the distance is immense and it is so much the greater for the pupil because he is faced with it during the first stages of his instruction. If deaf mutes are not held back at this point the reason is that, of all children, they are the most attentive and the most observing. Accustomed from their earliest childhood to hear and speak with their eyes, they have more practice than anyone else in the recognition of relations between visible objects. It was necessary then to look for a method more in keeping with the still torpid faculties of our young savage, a method by which the surmounting of each difficulty prepared him for a still more difficult task. It was in this spirit that I outlined my new plan. I will not stop to analyze it; it can be judged by its execution.

Upon a board, two feet square, I pasted three pieces of paper of very distinct shapes and decided colors. One was circular and red, another was triangular and blue, the third was square and black. By means of holes pierced in their centers and nails driven into the board, three pieces of cardboard of the same shapes and colors were placed there and left for some days upon their respective models pasted on the board. Then I lifted them and gave them to Victor and they were replaced without any difficulty. I assured myself by reversing the board and then changing the order of the figures, that this first result was not a matter of routine but was due to comparison. After some days I substituted another board for the first. I had pasted the same figures on it, but this time they were all of a uniform color. In the first case the pupil had the double indication of shapes and colors to aid him in recognition, in the second case he had only one guide, comparison of the shapes. At almost the same time I showed him a third where all the figures were the same but the colors different. The same tests always gave the same results, excepting that I do not count mistakes due to lack of attention. The facility with which he executed these easy comparisons obliged me to present some new ones to him. I made additions and modifications in the last two presentations. I added to the one with the different shaped figures some new shapes much less distinct and to the one with the colors some new colors which differed only in shade. There was, for example, in the first a rather long parallelogram besides a square, and in the second a pattern in sky blue beside one of grayish blue. He made some mistakes and showed some uncertainty about these, which disappeared after some days' practice.

These results emboldened me to new changes always more difficult. Each day I added, curtailed, and modified, provoking new comparisons and new judgments. At length the multiplicity and the complications of these little exercises finished by fatiguing his attention and his docility. Then those motions of impatience and rage which broke out so violently at the beginning of his sojourn in Paris, and especially when he found himself shut in his room, reappeared in all their intensity. Notwithstanding this fact, it seemed to me that the time had come when it was necessary energetically to overcome these outbreaks and no longer to mitigate them by compliance. I believed, therefore, that I ought to resist them.

So, when disgusted with some task (of which, in truth, he could not understand the end, and of which it was very natural that he should weary), he would take the pieces of cardboard, throw them on the ground with vexation and make for his bed in a fury. I let one or two minutes pass. I came again to my charge with as much *sang froid* as possible. I made him gather up all the cards scattered in his room and gave him no rest until they were properly replaced.

My persistence lasted only for a few days and was finally overcome by his independence of character. His fits of anger became more frequent, more violent, and were like the fits of madness of which I have already spoken but with this striking difference, that their effect was less directed towards persons than towards things. On such occasions he ran away and in a destructive mood bit the sheets, the blankets, and the mantelpiece, scattered the andirons, ashes and blazing embers, and ended by falling into convulsions which like those of epilepsy, involved a complete suspension of the sensorial functions. I was obliged to give up when things reached this frightful pitch; but my acquiescence only increased the evil. The paroxysms became more frequent, and apt to be renewed at the slightest opposition, often, even, without any determining cause.

My embarrassment became extreme. I foresaw the time when all my care would result only in making an unhappy epileptic of this poor child. A few more fits and force of habit would fasten upon him one of the most terrible and least curable of diseases. It was necessary then to find a remedy immediately, not in medicines which are so often fruitless, nor in gentleness from which there was nothing more to hope, but in a method of shock [16] almost parallel to the one which Boerhaave had employed at the Hospital at Haarlem. I was convinced that if the first means I adopted should fail in its effect, the trouble would only be aggravated, and any other treatment of the same nature would become useless. In this firm conviction I chose the form which I believed would be most alarming to a creature who

[16] "procédé perturbateur." (tr.)

in his new existence had not yet experienced any kind of danger.

Some time previously when Madame Guérin was with him at the Observatory, she had taken him on the platform, which is, as is well known, very high. Scarcely had he come to within a short distance of the parapet when, seized with fright, trembling in every limb and his face covered with sweat, he returned to his governess, whom he dragged by the arm towards the door, becoming somewhat calmer only when he got to the foot of the stairs. What could be the cause of such fright? That is not what I wanted to know. It was enough for me to know the effect to make it serve my purpose. The occasion soon offered itself in the instance of a most violent fit, which was, I believe, caused by our resuming the exercises. Seizing the moment when the functions of the senses were not yet suspended, I violently threw back the window of his room which was situated on the fourth story and which opened perpendicularly on to a big stone court. I drew near him with every appearance of anger and seizing him forcibly by the haunches held him out of the window, his head directly turned towards the bottom of the chasm. After some seconds I drew him in again. He was pale, covered with a cold sweat, his eyes were rather tearful, and he still trembled a little, which I believed to be the effect of fear. I led him to his cards. I made him gather them up and replace them all. This was done, very slowly to be sure, and badly rather than well, but at least without impatience. Afterwards he went and threw himself on his bed and wept copiously.

This was the first time, at least to my knowledge, that he shed tears. It preceded the occasions of which I have already given an account, when the grief at leaving his nurse or the pleasure of finding her again made him weep. The account of these came first in my narrative because I have followed the plan of a methodical exposition of facts rather than one in chronological order.

This strange method succeeded, if not completely, at least sufficiently. If his distaste for work was not entirely overcome, at least it was much diminished, and ceased to be followed by such effects as those which I have just related.

On such occasions as when he was a little overtired or when he was forced to work at times set apart for his walks or his meals, he contented himself with giving signs of weariness and impatience, and uttering a plaintive murmur which ordinarily ended in tears.

This favorable change allowed us to take up again our course of exercises where we had broken it off. These I submitted to new modifications which were designed to stabilize his judgment still further. For the figures pasted on the board, which I have said were completely colored shapes representing geometrical figures, I substituted linear outlines of these same shapes. I also contented myself with indicating the colors by little irregular samples quite unlike the colored cards. I may say that these new difficulties were only a game to the child; a result which was sufficient for the end I had in mind when adopting this system of direct comparisons. The moment had come to replace this by another which was much more instructive and which would have presented insurmountable difficulties if the way had not been smoothed in advance by the success of the methods just used.

I ordered to be printed as a big character upon a piece of cardboard two inches square each of the twenty-four letters of the alphabet. I had an equal number of spaces cut in a plank a foot and a half square. Into these the pieces of cardboard could be inserted, without the use of paste, so that their places could be changed as required. I had an equal number of characters of the same dimensions made in metal. These were meant to be compared by the pupil with the printed letters, and were to be arranged in their corresponding places.

The first trial of this method was made, in my absence, by Madame Guérin. I was very much surprised on my return to learn from her that Victor distinguished all the characters and arranged them properly. He was immediately put to the test and performed his task without any mistake. Though delighted with such an immediate success I was still far from able to explain its cause, and it was only some days after that I discovered this by noting the way in which our pupil proceeded to make this arrangement. In order to make the work easier he devised of his own accord a little expedient which in this task allowed him to dispense with memory, comparison and judgment. As soon as the board was put between his hands, he did not wait until the metal letters were taken out of their places but he himself took them and piled them upon his hand, following the order of their arrangement so that the last letter, after all were taken from the board, was the first on the pile. He began with this and finished with the last of the pile, thus beginning the board at the end and proceeding always from right to left. Moreover, he was able to improve upon this procedure; for very often the pile collapsed, the characters fell out and he had to straighten everything up and put it in order by the unaided efforts of attention. So the twenty-four letters were arranged in four rows of six each, making it easier to lift them up by rows only, and even to replace them in the same way by taking letters from the second row only when the first was replaced.

I do not know whether he reasoned as I suppose, but at least it is certain that he executed the performance in the manner described. It was then a true routine, but a routine of his own invention, and one which was perhaps as much

to the credit of his intelligence as was a method of arrangement hit upon shortly afterwards to the credit of his discernment. It was not difficult to set him off by giving him
the characters pellmell whenever he was given the board.
At last, in spite of the frequent transpositions to which I
submitted the printed characters by changing their places,
in spite of insidious arrangements, such as the O beside the
C, the E beside the F, etc., his discrimination became in-
fallible. In exercising it upon all these letters, the end I had
in view was to prepare Victor for a primitive but correct
use of the letters, namely the expression of needs which can
only be made known by means of speech. Far from believing
that I was already so near this great step in his education.
I was led by the spirit of curiosity rather than the hope of
success to try the experiment which follows.

One morning when he was waiting impatiently for the
milk which he always had for breakfast, I carried to him
his board which I had specially arranged the evening before
with the four letters *L.A.I.T.* Madame Guérin, whom I had
warned, approached, looked at the letters and immediately gave me a cup of milk which I pretended to drink
myself. A moment after I approached Victor, gave him the
four letters that I had lifted from the board, and pointed to
it with one hand while in the other I held the jug full of
milk. The letters were immediately replaced but in inverted
order, so that they showed *T.I.A.L.* instead of *L.A.I.T.* I
indicated the corrections to be made by designating with
my finger the letters to transpose and the proper place of
each. When these changes had reproduced the sign, he was
allowed to have his milk.

It is difficult to believe that five or six similar attempts
were sufficient, not only to make him arrange methodically
the four letters of the word *Lait* but to give him the idea
of the connection between the word and the thing. At least

this is the justifiable inference from what happened a week later. One evening when he was ready to set out for the Observatory, he was seen to provide himself on his own initiative with the four letters in question, and to put them in his pocket; he had scarcely arrived at Citizen Lemeri's house, where as I previously said he goes every day for some milk, when he produced them and placed them on a table in such a way as to form the word *LAIT*

It was originally my intention here to recapitulate the facts scattered throughout this work, but I thought that such a summary would never have the weight of this last achievement. I state it, naked and stripped of all reflections, so to speak, so that it may mark in a more striking way the stage which we have reached and serve as a guarantee of future achievement. In the meantime the conclusion may be drawn from the greater part of my observations, and above all from those indicated in the last two sections, that the child known under the name of the *Savage of Aveyron* is endowed with the free use of all his senses; that he can compare, discern and judge, and finally apply all the faculties of his understanding to the objects related to his instruction. It is essential to note that these happy changes have occurred during the short space of nine months in a subject believed to be incapable of attention; and the conclusion will follow that his education is possible, if it is not even already guaranteed, by this early success, quite apart from any results which time may bring—time which in its unalterable course seems to give the child, in powers and development, all that it takes away from man in the decline of his life.[17]

[17] It remains for enlightened observers to come and convince themselves of the truth of these results. They alone can judge of the value of the facts by bringing to their examination a judicial spirit and a

And meanwhile what important consequences for the philosophic and natural history of the human race already follow from this first series of observations! If they are collected, methodically classified and correctly evaluated we shall have material proof of most important truths, truths which Locke and Condillac were able to discover by the power of their genius and the depth of their meditations alone. It has appeared to me at least that the following conclusions may be drawn:

(1) That man is inferior to a large number of animals in the pure state of nature,[18] a state of nullity and barbarism that has been falsely painted in the most seductive colors; a state in which the individual, deprived of the

knowledge of psychology. The appreciation of the mental state of our savage is more difficult than one would expect. Daily experience and acquired ideas tend to lead the judgment astray. Says Condillac in a very similar case, "If the habit we have formed of assisting ourselves by signs did not prevent us from noticing all we owe to them, *we should only have to put ourselves in the place of this young man in order to understand how little knowledge he could acquire;* but we always judge according to our own situation." For sound judgment it is necessary then in this case not to consider the child as seen during a single examination, but to observe and study him at different intervals at all times of the day, in all his pleasures, in the midst of his little exercises, etc. All these things are indispensable, but even so they are not sufficient unless, in order to establish an exact comparison between the present and the past, the *Savage of Aveyron* was actually seen during the first months of his stay in Paris. Those who did not see him there and who might see him now would find in him an almost ordinary child who can not speak. They would not be able to appreciate the distance which separates this "almost ordinary" creature from the *Savage of Aveyron*, as he was when first brought into the company of human beings; a distance apparently very slight but really immense when it is investigated and when one estimates the number of new deductions and acquired ideas necessary to attain these last results.

[18] If two children, a male and a female, were isolated during babyhood and if the same were done with two of the least intelligent species of animal, I do not doubt that the latter would show themselves much superior to the former in providing for their own needs and in attending both to their own preservation and to that of their young.

characteristic faculties of his kind, drags on without intelligence or without feelings, a precarious life reduced to bare animal functions.

(2) That the moral superiority said to be *natural* to man is only the result of civilization, which raises him above other animals by a great and powerful force. This force is the preëminent sensibility of his kind, an essential peculiarity from which proceed the imitative faculties and that continual urge which drives him to seek new sensations in new needs.

(3) That this imitative force, the purpose of which is the education of his organs and especially the apprenticeship of speech, and which is very energetic and very active during the first years of his life, rapidly wanes with age, with isolation, and with all the causes which tend to blunt the nervous sensibility; from which it results that the articulation of sounds, of all the effects of imitation unquestionably the most incomprehensible and the most useful, must encounter innumerable obstacles at any age later than that of early childhood.

(4) That in the most isolated savage as in the most highly civilized man, there exists a constant relation between ideas and needs; that the increasing multiplicity of the latter in the most civilized peoples should be considered as a great means of developing the human mind; so that a general proposition may be established, namely, that all causes accidental, local or political, which tend to augment or diminish the number of our desires, necessarily contribute to extend or to narrow the sphere of our knowledge and the domain of science, fine arts and social industry.

(5) That in the present state of our knowledge of physiology the progress of education can and ought to be illumined by the light of modern medicine which, of all the natural sciences, can help most powerfully towards the perfection of the human species by detecting the organic and intellectual peculiarities of each individual and determining therefrom what education ought to do for him and what society can expect from him.

There are still certain equally important considerations that I proposed to add to those already given; but the development which they would have required would overstep the boundaries and the plan of this short treatise. I have noticed besides in comparing my observations with the doctrines of some of our metaphysicians that I found myself in disagreement with them upon certain interesting points.

Consequently it devolves upon me to wait for more numerous and therefore more conclusive facts. A very similar reason has prevented me, when speaking of young Victor's varied development, from dwelling on the time of his puberty, which has shown itself almost explosively for some weeks, and the first phenomena of which cast much doubt upon the origin of certain tender emotions which we now regard as very "natural." Though here I have found it advisable to reserve judgment and conclusions; I am persuaded that it is impossible to allow too long a period for the ripening and subsequent confirmation of all considerations which tend to destroy those prejudices which are possibly venerable and those illusions of social life which are the sweeter because they are the most consoling.

A REPORT MADE TO HIS EXCELLENCY THE MINISTER OF THE INTERIOR [19]

My Lord:

TO speak of the *Wild Boy of Aveyron* is to revive a name which now no longer arouses any kind of interest; it is to recall a creature forgotten by those who merely saw him and disdained by those who have thought to pass judgment on him. As for me, who until now have limited myself to observing him and lavishing my care upon him, I am quite indifferent both to forgetfulness and to disdain. Supported by daily observations lasting for five years I now beg to make to your Excellency the report which you expect of me; to relate what I have seen and done; to reveal the present state of this young man, the long and difficult paths through which he has been led, and the obstacles which he has overcome as well as those which he has not been able to surmount. If, my Lord, all these details may appear scarcely worthy of your attention and the results much below your expectations, will your Excellency please believe as my excuse that without the formal command received from him, I might have enveloped in a profound silence and condemned to an eternal oblivion, certain labors of which the result shows the failure of the instructor, rather than the progress of the pupil. But, while judging myself impartially, I believe nevertheless that, without taking into consideration the aim which I had in view in this task

[19] This second report was transmitted to the Minister of the Interior on November 19th, 1806.

which I have voluntarily imposed upon myself, and considering the enterprise from a general point of view, it will not be, my Lord, without a certain satisfaction that you will see in the diverse experiments which I have made and the numerous observations that I have gathered, a collection of facts qualified to throw light on the history of medical philosophy, on the study of uncivilized man, and on the direction of certain systems of private education.

In order to appreciate the present state of the *Wild Boy of Aveyron*, his past condition must be brought to mind. To be judged fairly, this young man must only be compared with himself. Put beside another adolescent of the same age he is only an ill-favored creature, an outcast of nature as he was of society. But if one limits onself to the two terms of comparison offered by the past and present states of young Victor, one is astonished at the immense space which separates them; and one can question whether Victor is not more unlike the *Wild Boy of Aveyron* arriving at Paris, than he is unlike other individuals of his same age and species.

I will not recount in detail to you, Sir, the hideous picture of this man-animal as he was when he came out of his forests. In a short treatise which was printed some years ago and of which I have the honor to offer you a copy, I have depicted this extraordinary creature as he was described in a report made by a celebrated doctor to a learned society. I will only recall here that, after a long examination and numerous attempts the commission, of which this doctor was the recorder, could not succeed in fixing the child's attention for a moment and sought in vain to discover in his actions and decisions any act of intelligence or any evidence of sensibility. A stranger to that reflective process which is the first source of ideas, he gave attention to nothing because nothing made any lasting impression upon his senses. His eyes saw without noticing, his ears heard and did not listen; and the organ of touch, restricted to the mechanical operation of grasping objects, had never been used to verify their forms and existence. Such, in short, was the state of the physical and mental faculties of this child that he should be ranked not only in the lowest grade of his species but even at the lowest stage of the animals, and it may be said that in some measure he differed from a plant only in that he had, in addition, the ability to move and utter cries. Between this less-than-animal existence and the present state of young Victor there is a prodigious difference, which would appear even more glaring if, suppressing all intermediate progress, I were merely to bring together the two extremes of the comparison. But I am persuaded that the important point is much less to contrast these two pictures than to give a faithful and complete account, and I shall therefore use every care to make known concisely all the changes that have occurred in the state of the young savage; and that there may be more order and interest in the enumeration of the facts, I will relate them in three distinct series relative to the triple development of the functions of the senses, the intellectual functions, and the emotional faculties.

First Series:

DEVELOPMENT OF THE FUNCTIONS OF THE SENSES

I. We are indebted to the works of Locke and Condillac for a just estimation of the powerful influence that the isolated and simultaneous action of our senses exerts upon the formation and development of our ideas. The abuse that has been made of this discovery destroys neither its truth nor the practical applications that can be made of it to a system of medical education. These were the principles I followed, when, after completing the main projects which I had first proposed and which are made known in my first work, I devoted all my attention to the exercise and individual development of young Victor's sense organs.

II. As of all the senses hearing is the one which contributes most particularly to the development of our intellectual faculties, I put all imaginable resources into play in order to awaken the ears of our savage from their long torpor. I was convinced that in order to educate this sense it was necessary in some measure to isolate it. In his whole organization I had at my disposition only a modicum of sensibility. I had therefore to concentrate this upon the sense that I wished to put into play by artificially paralyzing the sense of sight, the most important channel of this sensibility. Consequently I covered his eyes with a thick bandage and made the loudest and most varied noises in his ears. My intention was not only to make him hear these but also to make him listen to them. To obtain this result, when I had made a noise I induced Victor to make another like it by striking the same sonorous body, and to strike a different one as soon as his ear warned him that I had changed the instrument.

The aim of my first efforts was to make him distinguish the sound of a bell from that of a drum. Just as I had previously led him from the larger comparison of two pieces of cardboard, differently shaped and colored, to the distinction between letters and words, I had every reason to believe that the ear, following the same progression of attention as the sense of sight, would soon distinguish the most similar and the most different tones of the vocal organ. Consequently, I set myself to render the sounds progressively more alike, more complicated, and nearer together. Later I was not content with requiring him to merely distinguish the sound of a bell from that of a drum, but introduced the differences of sound produced by striking with a rod upon the skin, the hoop or body of a drum, or upon the bell of a clock, or a fire shovel, making a ringing noise.

III. Afterwards I adapted this comparative method to the perception of the tones of a wind instrument, which, more like those of the voice, formed the last step of the progression by means of which I hoped to induce my pupil to hear the different intonations of the larynx. Success followed my expectations and as soon as the sound of my voice struck the ears of our savage I found his ear sensitive to the slightest intonations.

IV. In these last experiments I could not, as in those preceding, require my pupil to repeat the sounds which he perceived. By dividing his attention this double task would have proved foreign to my plan, which was to educate each of his sense organs separately. I therefore required merely that the sounds should be perceived. To make certain of this, I placed my pupil opposite me, his eyes bandaged, his hands closed, and made him raise a finger every time I made a sound. This means of testing was well understood. The sound had scarcely struck his ear when his finger was raised with a kind of impetuosity, and often even with demonstrations of delight which did not permit any doubt as to the pleasure which the pupil found in these odd lessons. Whether it was that he took genuine pleasure in hearing the sound of the human voice, or merely that he had finally overcome the ennui of being deprived of light for long hours, I have more than once seen him, in the intervals between these exercises, come to me, his bandage in his hand, and, applying it himself to his eyes, stamp with joy when he felt my hands tie it firmly behind his head. It was only in these last experiments that such evidences of delight appeared. I immediately congratulated myself and far from repressing them, I even excited them without thinking that I was thus preparing an obstacle which before long would interrupt the series of these useful experiments and to annul some of the results that had been so laboriously obtained.

V. After I had assured myself by means of the method I have just described that Victor perceived all the sounds of the voice whatever their degree of intensity, I devoted myself to the task of making him compare them. It was no longer a question of merely recognizing the sounds of the voice, but of seizing upon their differences and of appreciating all the modifications and variations of tone which make up the music of speech. Between this and the preceding effort there was a tremendous distance for a creature who could develop only by carefully graduated steps and who advanced towards civilization only because I led him on imperceptibly. Upon encountering the difficulty which now presented itself, I resolved to show more patience and gentleness than ever. I was still further encouraged by the hope that once this obstacle was overcome, the education of the sense of hearing would be completed. We began by comparing the vowels, still using the hand to confirm the result of our experiments. Each of the five fingers was used to indicate one of the five vowels and to signify that it had been distinctly perceived. Thus the thumb represented A and had to be raised at the pronunciation of that vowel; the index finger E, the middle finger I, and so on.

VI. It was not without difficulty and much delay that I succeeded at last in giving him a distinct idea of the vowels. The first that he distinguished clearly was O, next the vowel A. The other three presented greater difficulty and for a long time he confused them. Finally, however, his ear began to perceive them as distinct. This was the time of which I have already spoken when those demonstrations of delight reappeared in all their liveliness and momentarily interrupted our new experiments. But as these distinctions required of the pupil a very sustained attention, delicate comparisons and repeated judgments, the result was that the expressions of delight which until now had only enlivened our lessons, came finally to disturb them. At such times he confused all the sounds and raised his fingers indiscriminately, frequently all together and with disorderly haste and decidedly impatient bursts of laughter. In order to repress this inopportune gaiety I tried giving back to my too hilarious pupil the use of his sight. I pursued our experiments in this way at the same time intimidating him with a severe and even somewhat menacing attitude. This increased his delight, but at the same time afforded continual distractions to the sense of hearing, inasmuch as all the objects which surrounded him engaged his sense of sight. The slightest alteration in the position of the furniture or in his clothes, the least movement of the people about him, a rather sudden change in the light of sun, all attracted his eye and were sufficient to distract his attention.

I again put the bandage on his eyes and the bursts of laughter were repeated. I then tried to intimidate him by my behavior since I could no longer hold him by my expression. I took one of the drum sticks which we had used in an experiment and struck him lightly upon the fingers when he made mistakes. He treated this as a joke and in his glee became even livelier. In order to undeceive him I thought it ncessary to make the punishment a little severer. He understood me, and it was with a mixture of pleasure and pain that I saw in the lad's clouded expression how the pain of the blow was lost in the feeling of insult. Tears rolled down from under his bandage. I hastened to raise it but whether from perplexity or fear or from a profound preoccupation of the inner senses, he persisted in keeping his eyes closed although freed of the bandage. I cannot describe how unhappy he looked with his eyes thus closed and with tears escaping from them every now and then. Oh! how ready I was on this occasion, as on many others, to give up my self-imposed task and regard as wasted the time that I had already given to it! How many times did I regret ever having known this child, and freely condemn the sterile and inhuman curiosity of the men who first tore him from his innocent and happy life!

VII. This scene put an end to the noisy gaiety of my pupil. But I had no reason to be pleased with my success and escaped from this embarrassment only to fall into another. A feeling of fear took the place of this foolish merriment and our exercises were more disturbed than ever. When I uttered a sound I was obliged to wait more than a quarter of an hour for the signal agreed upon. Even then, though correct it was made slowly and with such uncertainty that if, by accident, I made the least noise or the slightest movement, Victor would suddenly close his finger again in fear and raise another with the same slowness and circumspection. Yet I did not despair, but flattered myself this time, much kindness and gentle encouragement would dissipate this timesome and excessive timidity. I hoped in vain. All was useless. Thus vanished the brilliant expectations which I had founded, with some reason perhaps, upon an uninterrupted chain of interesting and useful experiments. Several times since, at periods widely separated, I have attempted the same tests and have seen myself obliged to give them up again, always blocked by the same obstacle.

VIII. Nevertheless this series of experiments upon the sense of hearing was not altogether useless. Victor owes to it the fact that he can distinguish words of one syllable, and above all, when presented with the different intonations of the language, can recognize with considerable accuracy those which are the expression of reproach, anger, sadness, contempt and sympathy, even when these various emotions are not accompanied by a corresponding play of the features or by such natural pantomimes as constitute their outward expression.

IX. Grieved rather than discouraged at the meager success obtained upon the sense of hearing I determined to devote all my efforts to the sense of sight. My first labors had improved this to a considerable degree and had contributed so much towards giving him stability and power of attention that at the time of my first report my pupil was already able to distinguish the metal letters and place them in the order necessary to form certain words. From this point to the distinct perception of written signs and even to the mechanism of writing, there was still a great distance; but happily all these difficulties disappeared by the use of the same plan. Thus they were easily overcome. At the end of some months my pupil could read and write passably well a series of words, several of which differed very little from one another and could be distinguished only by an attentive eye. But this reading conveyed no meaning to him. Victor read the words without pronouncing them and without understanding their significance. Even though little attention be paid to this kind of reading, the only kind, indeed, practicable for such a creature, the question will certainly be asked, how I could be sure that such words which were not pronounced and to which he attached no meaning, were distinctly read and not confused with one another. Nothing was simpler than the procedure which I employed to make certain of this. All the words given to be read were written upon two blackboards. I took one of them and turned the other towards Victor; then, pointing successively with my finger to all the words which were on the blackboard between my hands, I required him to show me the counterpart of each word indicated. I was careful to follow an entirely different order in the arrangement of the words so that the position of a word on one blackboard gave no indication whatever of its position on the other. Consequently, it was necessary to examine the individual appearance of all the signs to ensure their recognition at first glance.

X. When the pupil was misled by the appearance of a word and designated another in its place, I did not call attention to his error but made him rectify it merely by requiring him to spell the word. To spell was for us to compare mentally, one after the other, all the letters which made up the two words. This examination which was really of an analytical nature was made very rapidly. I touched the first letter of the other word with the end of a bodkin; from this we passed to the second and continued thus until Victor, always trying to find in his word the letters which I showed him in mine, succeeded in discovering the first letter which was different in the two words.

XI. Soon it was no longer necessary to use such a detailed examination to induce him to rectify his mistakes. It was enough to have him look attentively for a moment at the mistaken word to sense the difference and I might add that the error was corrected almost as soon as indicated. Thus I exercised and improved this important sense, whose lack of direction had caused the failure of the first attempts to fixate it and had brought about the first suspicions of idiocy.

XII. Having thus terminated the education of his sense of sight, I turned my attention to his sense of touch. Although far from sharing the opinion of Buffon and Condillac regarding the importance of the rôle played by this sense, I did not consider wasted any care which I might give to it, nor without interest such observations as its development might furnish. It has been seen in my first memoir that this sense, in its most primitive form limited to a mechanical grasping of bodies, was developed by means of hot baths to a point where, among other qualities, heat and cold, roughness and smoothness were perceived. But if attention is given to the nature of these two qualities of sensation it will be seen that they belong to all parts of the skin alike. The special sense of touch had only received a share of the sensitiveness that I had awakened in the whole cutaneous system. Thus it functioned merely as part of that system, since it did not differ from the rest of it by any special functional peculiarities.

XIII. My first experiments confirmed the accuracy of this estimate. At the bottom of an opaque vase, the mouth of which would scarcely allow the introduction of an arm, I placed some cooked chestnuts which were still hot, and near them some chestnuts of the same size, but hollow and cold. One of my pupil's hands was in the vase and the other open upon his knee. Upon the open hand I placed a hot chestnut and told Victor to get me one from the bottom of

the vase. This he did. I gave him a cold chestnut. The one
he took out of the vase was also cold. I repeated this experiment several times, always successfully. The result was
different when, instead of making him compare the temperature of the thing, I wished by the same exploratory means
to make him judge of the shape. There the exclusive function
of touch began to operate, and that sense was still untrained.
I put some chestnuts and acorns in the vase and when I
showed one or the other of these to Victor, and wanted him
to bring me a similar one from the bottom of the vessel, he
would bring an acorn for a chestnut or a chestnut for an
acorn. It was necessary then to induce this sense to function
by using the method adopted with all the other senses.
To this effect I gave him practice in comparing objects very
dissimilar not only in shape but also in size, such as a stone
and a chestnut, a penny and a key. It was not without
trouble that I succeeded in making him distinguish these
objects by touch. When he no longer confused them I replaced them by others less unlike, such as an apple, a nut,
and some little pebbles. I afterwards submitted to this
manual examination the chestnuts and the acorns and this
comparison was now no more than child's play. Thence I
reached the point where he distinguished in the same way
even the most similar metal letters, such as B and R, I and
J, C and G.

XIV. This kind of exercise from which, as I have already
said, I did not promise myself much success, nevertheless
contributed not a little towards increasing our pupil's power
of attention. On other occasions I have seen his feeble intelligence endeavor to overcome much more obstinate difficulties, but never have I seen him assume the serious, calm,
and meditative air which spread over his whole face when
he made up his mind about the difference of shape in the
object submitted to this tactual examination.

XV. It now remained for me to apply myself to the sense of taste and smell. This last was of an unsurpassable delicacy. It is known that long after this young man was living in a civilized community he still had the habit of sniffing at everything that was given to him, even such things as we consider without smell. During the country walks which I often took with him in his first months at Paris, I have many times seen him stop, and even turn round, to pick up pebbles and bits of dried wood, which he threw away only after holding them to his nose, often with the appearance of great satisfaction. One evening when he had wandered in the Rue d'Enfer and was only found by his governess after nightfall, it was only after sniffing at her hands and arms two or three times that he made up his mind to follow her, letting his delight burst forth at having found her again. Civilization could then add nothing to the delicacy of his sense of smell. Moreover, being much more closely bound up with the exercise of the digestive functions than with the development of the intellectual faculties, this sense did not enter into my plan of instruction. It might appear that the sense of taste, being in general connected with the same functions as that of smell, would be equally foreign to my purpose. I did not think so, because I considered the sense of taste not from the point of view of the very limited function which nature has assigned to it, but in relation to the delights, as varied as they are numerous, of which civilization has made it the organ. Accordingly, I was forced to conclude that it was worth while to develop or rather pervert it. I believe it useless here to enumerate all the expedients to which I resorted in order to attain this end and by means of which I succeeded in a very short time in awakening the taste of our savage to many dishes which, until then, he had always disdained. Nevertheless, among these fresh acquisitions of the senses Victor did not show any of those greedy preferences which constitute gluttony. Very different from those men called savages who live in a half degree of civilization and who show all the vices of large communities and none of their virtues, Victor, while becoming accustomed to new dishes, has remained indifferent to strong drinks, and this indifference developed into aversion after a mistake the effect and circumstances of which are perhaps worth describing.

Victor was dining with me in town. At the end of the meal, on his own initiative, he took up a decanter containing one of the strongest cordials but which, since it had neither color nor odor, looked exactly like water. Our savage took it for such, poured out half a glassful and, no doubt because he was very thirsty, suddenly drank nearly half of it before the burning which it caused in his stomach warned him of his mistake. Then throwing down suddenly glass, spirits, and all, he sprang up furious, made a single leap from his place to the door of his room, and ran howling backwards and forwards in the corridors and up and down the staircases of the house over and over again; he was like an animal who has been badly wounded, and who in the rapidity of his course does not, as the poets say, seek to flee from the arrow which tears him, but tries by violent movement to divert a pain, to the alleviation of which it cannot, as man does, call a beneficent hand.

XVI. Yet in spite of his aversion to spirits Victor has acquired a certain liking for wine, without appearing, however, to feel very much its privation if it is not given him. I even believe that he has always retained a marked preference for water. The way in which he drinks it seems to show that it gives him the keenest delight, but this is due no doubt to some cause other than the pleasures of the sense of taste. At the end of his dinner, even when he is no longer thirsty, he is always seen with the air of an epicure who holds his glass for some exquisite liquor, to fill his glass with pure water, take it by sips and swallow it drop by drop. But what adds much interest to this scene is the place where it occurs. It is near the window with his eyes turned towards the country, that our drinker stands, as if in this moment of happiness this child of nature tries to unite the only two good things which have survived the loss of his liberty—a drink of limpid water and the sight of sun and country.

XVII. Thus the improvement of his senses was effected. With the exception of hearing, all these emerged from their long torpor [20] and opened up to new perceptions, bearing to the soul of our young savage many ideas until then unknown. But these ideas left only a fugitive trace in his brain and in order to fix them it was necessary to impress on his mind their respective signs or rather the meaning of these signs. The signs Victor knew because I had already combined the perception of the objects and their visible qualities with the reading of the words representing them, without trying, however, to determine the meaning of the latter. Victor, taught to distinguish by touch a round thing from a flat thing; by his eyes, a red paper from a blue paper, and by taste, an acid liquid from a sweet liquid, had at the same time learned to distinguish from each other the words which express the different perceptions, but without knowing the representative value of the signs. As this knowledge no longer belonged to the domain of the external senses, it was necessary to appeal to the faculties of the mind and, if I may so express myself, to ask of him that he produce an account of the ideas that these senses had furnished. It is this which became the object of a new set of experiments which form the material of the following series.

[20] Reading *hébétude* (tr.).

Second Series:

DEVELOPMENT OF THE INTELLECTUAL FUNCTIONS

XVIII. Although presented separately, the facts which have just been related are connected in many ways with those which will form the subject matter of the following sections. For such, my Lord, is the intimate relation which unites physical with intellectual man that, although their respective provinces appear and are in fact very distinct; yet the borderline between the two different sorts of function is very confused.

Their development is simultaneous and their influence reciprocal. Thus while I was limiting my efforts to the exercise of the senses of our savage, the mind took its share of the attention given exclusively to the education of these organs and followed the same order of development. In fact it seemed that in instructing the senses to perceive and to distinguish new objects, I forced the attention to fix itself on them, the judgment to compare them, and the memory to retain them. Thus nothing was immaterial in these exercises. Everything penetrated to the mind. Everything put the faculties of the intelligence into play and prepared them for the great work of the communication of ideas. I was already sure that this would be possible by leading the pupil to the point where he would designate the thing he wanted by means of letters arranged in such a way as to spell the name of the thing he desired. In my pamphlet upon this child I have given an account of the first step

67

made in recognizing written signs, and I am not afraid to signalize it as an important epoch in his education, as the sweetest and most brilliant success that has ever been obtained upon a creature fallen as was this one, into the lowest extremity of brutishness. But subsequent observations, by throwing light upon the nature of this result, soon came to weaken the hopes that I had conceived from it. I noticed that Victor did not use words which I had taught him for the purpose of asking for the objects, or of making known a wish or a need, but employed them at certain moments only, and always at the sight of the desired things. Thus for example, much as he wanted his milk it was only at the moment when he was accustomed to take it and at the actual instant when he saw that it was going to be given him that the word for this favorite food was expressed or rather formed in the proper way. In order to clear up the suspicion that this restricted employment of the words awoke in me I tried delaying the hour of his breakfast but waited in vain for the written expression of my pupil's needs although they had become very urgent. It was not until the cup appeared that the word *lait* (milk) was formed. I resorted to another test. In the middle of his lunch and without letting it appear in any way to be a punishment, I took away his cup of milk and shut it up in a cupboard. If the word *lait* had been for Victor the distinct sign of the thing and the expression of his want of it, there is no doubt that after this sudden privation, the need continuing to make itself felt, the word would have been immediately produced. It was not, and I concluded that the formation of this sign, instead of being for the pupil the expression of his desire, was merely a sort of preliminary exercise with which he mechanically preceded the satisfaction of his appetite. It was necessary then to retrace our steps and begin again. I resigned myself courageously to do this, believing that if I had not been understood by my pupil it was my fault rather than his. Indeed, in reflecting upon the causes which might give rise to this defective reception of the written signs, I recognized that in these first examples of the expression of ideas I had not employed the extreme simplicity which I had introduced at the beginning of my other methods of instruction and which had insured their success. Thus although the word *lait* is for us only a simple sign, for Victor it might be a confused expression for the drink, the vessel which contained it, and the desire of which it was the object.

XIX. Several other signs with which I had familiarized him showed the same lack of precision in application. An even more considerable defect was inherent in the method of expression we had adopted. As I have already said, this consisted in placing metal letters on a line and in the proper order, in such a way as to form the name of each object. But the connection which existed between the thing and the word was not immediate enough for his complete apprehension. In order to do away with this difficulty, it was necessary to establish between each object and its sign a more direct connection and a sort of identity which fixed them simultaneously in his memory. The objects first submitted to a trial of this new method of expression had therefore to be reduced to the greatest simplicity, so that their signs could not in any way bear upon their accessories. Consequently I arranged on the shelves of a library several simple objects such as a pen, a key, a knife, a box, etc., each one on a card upon which its name was written. These names were not new to the pupil. He already knew them and had learned to distinguish them from each other, according to the method of reading which I have already indicated.

XX. The problem then was merely to familiarize his eyes with the respective display of each of these names under the object which it represented. This arrangement was soon grasped as I had proof when, displacing all the things and instantly replacing all the labels in another order, I saw the pupil carefully replace each object upon its name. I varied my tests, and the variation gave me the opportunity to make several observations relative to the degree of the impression which these written signs made upon the sensory apparatus of our savage. Thus, leaving all the things in one corner of the room and taking all the labels to another, I wished by showing them successively to Victor to make him fetch each thing for which I showed him the written word. On these occasions, in order for him to bring the thing it was necessary that he should not lose from sight for a single instant the characters which indicated it. If he was too far away to be able to read the label, or if after showing it to him thoroughly I covered it with my hand, from the moment the sight of the word escaped him he assumed an air of uneasiness and anxiety and seized at random the first object which chanced to his hand.

XXI. The result of this experiment was not very reassuring and would in fact have discouraged me completely if I had not noticed that after frequent repetitions the duration of the impression upon the brain of my pupil became by imperceptible degrees much longer. Soon he merely needed to glance quickly at the word I showed him, in order to go without haste or mistake to fetch the thing I asked for. After some time I was able to extend the experiment by sending him from my apartment into his own room to look in the same way for anything the name of which I showed him. At first the duration of the perception did not last nearly so long as that of the journey, but by an act of intelligence worthy of record, Victor sought and found in the agility of his legs a sure means of making the impressions persist longer than the time required for the journey. As soon as he had thoroughly read the word he set out like an arrow, coming back an instant later with the thing in his hand. More than once, nevertheless, the name escaped him on the way. Then I heard him stop in his tracks and come again towards my apartment, where he arrived with a timid and confused air. Sometimes it was enough for him to glance at the complete collection of names in order to recognize and retain the one which had escaped him. At other times the image of the word was so effaced from his memory that I was obliged to show it to him afresh. This necessity he indicated by taking my hand and making me pass my index finger over the whole series of names until I had shown him the forgotten one.

XXII. This exercise was followed by another which by offering his memory more work contributed more powerfully to develop it. Until then I had limited myself to asking for only one thing at a time. Then I asked for two, then three, and then four by showing a similar number of the labels to the pupil. He, feeling the difficulty of retaining them all, did not stop running over them with eager attention until I had entirely screened them from his eyes. Then there was no more delay or uncertainty. He set off hurriedly on the way to his room whence he brought the things requested. On his return his first care before giving them to me was to look hastily over the list, comparing it with the things of which he was the bearer. These he gave me only after he had reassured himself in this way that he had neither forgotten anything nor made a mistake. This last experiment gave at first very variable results but finally the difficulties which it offered were in their turn surmounted. The pupil, now sure of his memory, disdained the advantage which the agility of his legs gave him and applied himself quietly to this exercise. He often stopped in the corridor, put his face to the window which is at one end of it, greeted with sharp cries the sight of the country which unfolds magnificently in the distance, and then set off again for his room, got his little cargo, renewed his homage to the ever-regretted beauties of nature, and returned to me quite sure of the correctness of his errand.

XXIII. In this way memory, reëstablished in all its functions, succeeded in retaining the symbols of thought while at the same time the intelligence fully grasped their importance. Such, at least, was the conclusion that I thought I could draw when I constantly saw Victor, wishing to ask for various things, either in our exercises or spontaneously, making use of the different words of which I had taught him the meaning by the device of showing or giving him the thing when we made him read the word, or by indicating the word when he was given the thing. Who could believe that this double proof was not more than sufficient to assure me that at last I had reached the point to gain which I had been obliged to retrace my steps and make so great a detour? But something happened at this juncture which made me believe for a moment that I was further from it than ever.

XXIV. One day when I had taken Victor with me and sent him as usual to fetch from his room several objects which I had indicated upon his list of words, it came into my head to double-lock the door and unseen by him to take out the key. That done I returned to my study, where he was, and, unrolling his list, I asked him for some of the things on it, taking care to indicate none which were not also to be found in my room. He set out immediately, but finding the door locked and having searched on all sides for the key, he came beside me, took my hand and led me to the outer door as if to make me see that it would not open. I feigned surprise and sought for the key everywhere and even pretended to open the door by force. At last, giving up the vain attempt, I took Victor back into my study and showing him the same words again, invited him by signs to look about and see if there were not similar objects to be found there. The words designated were stick, bellows, brush, glass, knife. All these things were to be found scattered about my study in places where they could easily be seen. Victor looked at them but touched none of them. I had no better success in making him recognize them when they were brought together on a table and it was quite useless to ask for them one after the other by showing him successively their names. I tried another method. With scissors I cut out the names of the objects, thus converting them into single labels which were put into Victor's hands. By thus bringing him back to our original procedure, I hoped that he would put upon each thing the name which represented it. In vain. I had the inexpressible grief of seeing my pupil unable to recognize any of these objects or rather the connection which joined them to their signs. With a stupefied air which cannot be described he let his heedless glance wander over all these characters which had again become unintelligible. I felt myself sinking under a weight of impatience and discouragement.

I went and sat at the end of the room and considered bitterly this unfortunate creature reduced by the strangeness of his lot to such sad alternatives. Either he must be relegated as an unmistakable idiot to one of our asylums, or he must, by unheard-of labor, procure a little education which would be just as little conducive to his happiness. "Unhappy creature," I cried as if he could hear me, and with real anguish of heart, "since my labors are wasted and your efforts fruitless, take again the road to your forests and the taste for your primitive life. Or if your new needs make you dependent on a society in which you have no place, go, expiate your misfortune, die of misery and boredom at Bicêtre."

Had I not known the range of my pupil's intelligence so well, I could have believed that I had been fully understood, for scarcely had I finished speaking when I saw his chest heave noisily, his eyes shut, and a stream of tears escape through his closed eyelids, with him the signs of bitter grief.

XXV. I had often noticed that when such emotions had reached the point of tears, they formed a kind of salutary crisis that suddenly developed the intelligence which immediately afterwards was often able to overcome a difficulty that had appeared insurmountable some moments before. I had also observed that if at the height of this emotion I suddenly left off reproaching him and substituted caresses and a few words of affection and encouragement, I obtained an increase of emotion which doubled the expected effect. The occasion was favorable and I hastened to profit by it. I drew near to Victor. I made him listen to a few kind words which I spoke in such terms as he could understand and which I accompanied by evidences of affection still more intelligible. His tears redoubled and were accompanied by gasps and sobs, while I myself redoubled the caresses, raising his emotion to the highest intensity and causing him, if I may thus express myself, to vibrate to the last sensitive fiber of his mentality. When all this excitement had entirely calmed down I placed the same objects again under his eyes, and induced him to indicate them one after the other as soon as I successively showed him the names. I began by asking him for the book. He first looked at it for rather a long time, made a movement towards it with his hand while trying to detect in my eyes some signs of approval or disapproval which would settle his uncertainty. I held myself on guard and my expression was blank. Reduced then to his own judgment he concluded that it was not the thing asked for, and his eyes wandered, looking on all sides of the room, pausing, however, only at the books which were scattered upon the table and mantelpiece.

This examination was like a flash of light to me. I immediately opened a cupboard which was full of books and took out a dozen among which I was careful to include one exactly like the one Victor had left in his room. To see it, quickly carry his hand to it and give it to me with a radiant air was for Victor only the affair of a moment.

XXVI. Here I stopped the experiment. The result was enough to revive the hopes which I had too easily abandoned and to make clear to me the difficulties which this experiment had brought to light. It was evident that my pupil, far from having conceived a wrong idea of the meaning of the symbols, had only made too rigorous an application of them. He had taken my lessons too literally and as I had limited myself to giving him the nomenclature of certain things in his room he was convinced that these were the only things to which it was applicable. Thus every book which was not the one he had in his room was not a book for Victor, and before he could decide to give it the same name it was necessary that an exact resemblance should establish a visible identity between the one and the other. This is a very different procedure in nomenclature from that of children, who, when beginning to speak, give to particular terms the value of general ones but keep the restricted meaning of the particular term.[21]

What could account for this strange difference? If I am not mistaken it grew out of an unusual acuteness of visual observation which was the inevitable result of the special education given to his sense of sight. By the method of analytical comparison I had trained this sense organ so thoroughly in the recognition of the visible qualities of

---

[21] E.g., a child calling all men daddy (particular term) will really think of them all as father (tr.).

objects and the differences of dimension, color and conformation, that he could always detect between two identical things such points of dissimilarity as would make him believe there was an essential difference between them. With the source of the error thus located, the remedy became easy. It was to establish the identity of the objects by demonstrating to the pupil the identity of their uses or their properties. It was to make him see common qualities which earned the same name for things apparently different. In a word, it was a question of teaching him to consider things no longer with reference to their differences but according to their similarities.

XXVII. This new study was a kind of introduction to the act of comparison. At first the pupil gave himself up to it so completely that he was inclined to go astray again by attaching the same idea and giving the same name to things which had no other connection than the conformity of their shapes or uses. Thus under the name of book he indicated indiscriminately a handful of paper, a note book, a newspaper, a register, a pamphlet. All straight and long pieces of wood were called sticks. At one time he gave the name of brush to the broom, and at another that of broom to the brush, and soon, if I had not repressed this abuse of comparison, I should have seen Victor restricted to the use of a small number of signs which he would have applied indiscriminately to a large number of entirely different things which had only certain general qualities or properties in common.

XXVIII. In the midst of these mistakes, or rather fluctuations, of an intelligence tending ceaselessly to inaction but continually provoked by artificial means, there apparently developed one of those characteristic faculties of man, and especially thinking man, the faculty of invention. When considering things from the point of view of their similarity or of their common qualities, Victor concluded that since there was a resemblance of shape between certain objects, there ought in certain circumstances to be an identity of uses and functions. Without doubt this conclusion was somewhat risky. But it gave rise to judgments which, even though obviously found to be defective, became so many new means to instruction. I remember that one day when I asked him in writing for a knife, he looked for one for some time and contented himself with offering me a razor, which he fetched from a neighboring room. I pretended it would do and when his lesson was finished gave him something to eat as usual. I wanted him to cut his bread instead of dividing it with his fingers as was his custom. And to this end I held out to him the razor which he had given me under the name of knife. His behavior was consistent, he tried to use it as such, but the lack of stability of the blade prevented this. I did not consider the lesson complete. I took the razor and, in the actual presence of Victor, made it serve its proper use. From then on the instrument was no longer and could not be any longer in his eyes a knife. I longed to make certain. I again took his book and showed him the word *couteau* (knife) and the pupil immediately showed me the object he held in his hand and which I had given him a moment ago when he could not use the razor. To make the result convincing it was necessary to reverse the test. If the book were put in Victor's hands while I touched the razor, it was necessary that he should fail to pick out any word, as he did not yet know the name of this instrument. He passed this test also.

XXIX. At other times his substitutions were evidence of much more bizarre comparisons. One day when he was dining in town he wished to receive a spoonful of lentils offered him at a moment when there were no more plates and dishes on the table, I remember that he had the idea of going and taking from the mantelpiece and holding it out as if it were a plate, a little circular picture under glass, set in a frame, the smooth and projecting edge of which made it not at all unlike a plate.

XXX. But very often his expedients were happier, more successful and better deserving the name of invention. Quite worthy of such a name was the way by which he provided himself one day with a pencil case. Only once in my study had I made him use one to hold a small piece of chalk too short to take up with the end of his fingers. A few days afterwards the same difficulty occurred again but Victor was in his room and had no pencil-holder at hand to hold his chalk. I put it to the most industrious or the most inventive man to say, or rather do, what he did in order to procure one. He took an implement used in roasting, found in well-equipped kitchens but quite superfluous in one belonging to a poor creature such as he was, and which for that reason had remained forgotten and corroded with rust at the bottom of a little cupboard—namely a skewer. Such was the instrument which he took to replace the one he lacked and which by a further inspiration of really creative imagination he was clever enough to convert into a real pencil-holder by replacing the slide with a few turns of thread. Pardon, My Lord, the importance which I attach to this act. One must have experienced all the anguish of a course of instruction as painful as this had been; one must have followed and directed this man-plant in his laborious developments from the first act of attention up to this first spark of imagination before one can have any idea of the joy that I felt, and can pardon me for introducing at this moment, and with something of a flourish, so ordinary and so simple a fact. What also added to the importance of this result when considered as a proof of actual progress and as a guarantee of future improvement is that, instead of occurring as an isolated incident which might have made it appear accidental, it was one among many incidents, doubtless less striking, but which, coming at the same period and evidently emanating from the same source, appeared in the eyes of an attentive observer to be diverse results of a general impulse. It is, indeed, worthy of notice that from this moment many routine habits which the pupil had contracted when applying himself to the little occupations prescribed for him, spontaneously disappeared. While rigidly refraining from making forced comparisons or drawing remote conclusions, one may, I think, at least suspect that this new way of looking at familiar things which gave birth to the idea of making new applications of them, might be expected to have precisely the result of forcing the pupil out of the unvarying round of, so to speak, automatic habits.

XXXI. Thoroughly convinced at last that I had completely established in Victor's mind the connection of the objects with their signs, it only remained for me to increase the number gradually. If the procedure by which I established the meaning of the first signs has been thoroughly grasped it will be seen that it could be applied only to a limited number of objects and to things small in size, and that a bed, a room, a tree, or a person, as well as the constituent and inseparable parts of a whole, could not be labeled in the same way. I did not find any difficulty in making the sense of these new words understood, although I could not, as in the preceding experiments bind them visibly to the things they represented. In order to be understood it was sufficient for me to point to the new word with a finger and with the other hand to show the object to which the word belonged. I had little more trouble in making him understand the names of the parts which enter into the composition of the whole object. Thus for a long time the words fingers, hands, forearms could not offer any distinct meaning to the pupil. This confusion in attaching the signs was evidently due to the fact that he had not yet understood that the parts of a body considered separately formed in their turn distinct objects which had their particular names. In order to give him the idea I took a bound book, tore off its covers, and detached several of its leaves. As I gave Victor each of these separate parts I wrote its name upon the blackboard. Then taking from his hands the various pieces, I made him in turn indicate their names to me. When they were thoroughly engraved on his memory, I replaced the separated parts and when I again asked their names he indicated them as before; then showing him the whole book without indicating any part in particular, I asked him the name. He pointed to the word book.

XXXII. This is all that was necessary to render him familiar with the names of the various parts of compound bodies; and to avoid confusion between the names of the separate parts and the general name of the object, I was careful in my demonstrations to touch each part directly and, when applying the general name, to content myself with indicating the thing vaguely without touching it.

XXXIII. From this lesson I passed on to the qualities of the bodies. Here I entered into the field of abstractions and I entered it with the fear of not being able to penetrate or finding myself soon halted by insurmountable difficulties. None showed themselves, and my first lesson was grasped instantly although it bore upon one of the most abstract qualities, that of extension. I took two books of similar bindings but of different sizes, the one an octodecimo, the other an octavo. I touched the first. Victor opened his book and pointed to the word *book*. I touched the second. The pupil indicated the same word. I began again several times and always with the same result. Next I took the little book, and giving it to Victor, made him put his hand flat upon the cover which it hid almost entirely. I then made him do the same thing with the octavo volume; his hand covered scarcely half of it. So that he could not mistake my intention I showed him the part which remained uncovered, and induced him to stretch out his fingers towards this part which he could not do without uncovering a part equal to that which he covered. After this experiment which demonstrated in such a tangible manner to my pupil the difference in size of these two objects, I again asked him the name. Victor hesitated. He felt that the same name could no longer be applied indiscriminately to two things which he had just found so unequal. This was what I was waiting for. I wrote the word *book* upon two cards and placed one upon each book. I next wrote upon a third the word *big*, and the word *little* upon a fourth. I placed them beside the others, the one on the octavo and the other upon the small volume. Having made Victor notice this arrangement I took the labels again, mixed them several times, and then gave them to him to be replaced. This was done correctly.

XXXIV. Had I been understood? Had the respective sense of the words *big* and *little* been grasped? In order to be certain and to have complete proof, this is what I did. I got two nails of unequal length. I compared them in almost the same way as I had done with the books. Then having written upon two cards the word *nail* I gave them to him without adding the two adjectives big and little, hoping that if my preceding lesson had been thoroughly grasped he would apply to the nails the same signs of relative size as he had served to mark the difference of dimension of the two books. He did this with a promptness that rendered the proof still more conclusive. Such was the procedure by which I gave him the idea of size. I used it with the same success to render intelligible the signs which represent the other sensible qualities of bodies such as color, weight, resistance, etc.

XXXV. After the explanation of the adjective, came the verb. To make this understood by the pupil I had only to submit to several kinds of action an object of which he knew the name. These actions I designated as soon as executed, by the infinitive of the verb in question. For example I took a key and wrote its name upon the blackboard. Then *touching* it, *throwing* it, *picking* it up, *kissing* it, *putting* it back in its place, and so on, I simultaneously wrote in a column at the side of the word *key,* the verbs *to touch, to throw, to pick up, to kiss, to replace,* etc. For the word *key* I then substituted the name of another object which I submitted to the same functions, pointing at the same time to the verbs already written. It often happened that in thus replacing at random one object by another in order to have it governed by the same verbs, there was such an inconsistency between them and the nature of the object that the action asked for became odd or impossible. The embarrassment in which the pupil found himself generally turned out to his advantage as much as to my own satisfaction; for it gave him the chance to exercise his discernment and me the opportunity of gathering proofs of his intelligence. For example, when I found myself one day, after successive changes of the objects of the verbs, with such strange association of words as *to tear stone, to cut cup, to eat broom,* he evaded the difficulty very well by changing the two actions indicated by the first two verbs into others less incompatible with the nature of their objects. Thus he took a hammer to break the stone and dropped the cup to break it. Coming to the third verb (eat) and not being able to find any word to replace it, he looked for something else to serve as the object of the verb. He took a piece of bread and ate it.

In our study of these grammatical difficulties we were obliged to creep painfully and by endless detours, and so we simultaneously practised writing both as an auxiliary means of instruction and as a necessary diversion. As I had anticipated, the beginning of this work offered innumerable difficulties. Writing is an exercise in imitation, and imitation was yet to be born in our savage. Thus when for the first time I gave him a bit of chalk and arranged it conveniently in his fingers, I could obtain from him no line or stroke which might lead me to suspect any intention on the pupil's part to imitate what he had seen me do. Here then it was necessary once more to retrace our steps and to try and rouse from their inertia the imitative faculties by submitting them, as we had the others, to a kind of gradual education. I proceeded to the execution of this plan by practising Victor in the performance of acts when imitation is crude, such as lifting his arms, putting forward his foot, sitting down and getting up at the same time as myself; then opening his hand, shutting it, and repeating with his fingers many movements, first simple, then combined, that I performed in front of him. I next put into his hand, as in my own, a long rod sharpened to a point, and made him hold it as if it were a quill for writing, with the double intention of giving more strength and poise to his fingers through the difficulty of holding this imitation pen in equilibrium, and of making visible, and consequently capable of imitation, even the slightest movement of the rod.

XXXVII. Thus prepared by preliminary exercises we placed ourselves before the blackboard, each furnished with a piece of chalk, and placing our two hands at the same height I began by making a slow vertical movement towards the bottom of the board. The pupil did just the same, following exactly the same direction and dividing his attention between his line and mine, looking without intermission from the one to the other as if he wished to compare them successively at all points.

The result of our actions was two lines exactly parallel. My subsequent lessons were merely a development of the same procedure. I will not describe them. I will only say that the result was such that at the end of some months Victor could copy the words of which he already knew the meaning. Soon after he could reproduce them from memory, and finally make use of his writing, entirely unformed though it was and has remained, to express his wants, to solicit the means to satisfy them and to grasp by the same method of expression the needs or the will of others.

XXXVIII. In considering my experiments as a real course in imitation, I believed that the actions should not be limited to manual activity. I introduced several procedures which had no connection with the mechanism of writing but which were much more conducive to the exercise of intelligence. Such among others is the following. I drew upon a blackboard two circles almost equal, one opposite myself and the other in front of Victor. I arranged upon six or eight points of the circumference of these circles six or eight letters of the alphabet and wrote the same letters within the circles but disposed them differently. Next I drew several lines in one of the circles leading to the letters placed in the circumference. Victor did the same thing on the other circle. But because of the different arrangement of the letters, the most exact imitation nevertheless gave an entirely different figure from the one I had just offered as a model. Thence was to come the idea of a special kind of imitation which was not a matter of slavishly copying a given form but one of reproducing its spirit and manner without being held up by the apparent difference in the result. Here was no longer a routine repetition of what the pupil saw being done, such as can be obtained up to a certain point from certain imitative animals, but an intelligent and reasoned imitation, as variable in its method as in its applications, and in a word, such as one has a right to expect from a man endowed with the free use of all his intellectual faculties.

XXXIX. Of all the phenomena observable during the first developments of a child perhaps the most astonishing is the facility with which he learns to speak. When one thinks that speech, which is without question the most marvelous act of imitation, is also its first result, admiration is redoubled for that Supreme Intelligence whose masterpiece is man, and Who, wishing to make speech the principal promoter of education, could not let imitation, like the other faculties, develop progressively, and therefore necessarily made it fruitful as well as active from its beginning. But this imitative faculty, the influence of which extends throughout the whole of life, varies in its application according to age. It is used in learning to speak only during earliest childhood. Later other functions come under its influence and it abandons, so to speak, the vocal instrument, so that a young child, even an adolescent, after leaving his native country, promptly loses its manners, etiquette and language, but never loses those intonations of voice which constitute what is called accent. It follows from this physiological truth that in awakening the faculty of imitation in this young savage, now an adolescent, I ought not to have expected to find any disposition in the vocal organ to profit by this development of the imitative faculties, even supposing that I had not found a second obstacle in the obstinate lethargy of the sense of hearing. With respect to hearing, Victor could be considered as a deaf mute although he was certainly much inferior to this class of unfortunates since they are essentially observers and imitators.

XL. Nevertheless, I did not believe that I should allow this difference to bring me to a standstill or to let it deprive me of the hope of making him speak, with all the resulting advantages which I promised myself. I felt I should try a last resource, which was to lead him to the use of speech through the sense of sight, since it was out of the question to do so through the sense of hearing. Here the problem was to practise his eye in observing the mechanism of the articulation of sounds, and to practise his voice in the reproduction of the sounds by the use of a happy combination of attention and imitation. For more than a year all my work and all our exercises were directed towards this end. In order to follow the previous methods of insensible gradation, I preceded the study of the visible articulation of sounds by the slightly easier imitation of movements of the face muscles, beginning with those which were most easily seen. Thus we have instructor and pupil facing each other and grimacing their hardest; that is to say, putting the muscles of the eyes, forehead, mouth and jaw into all varieties of motion, little by little concentrating upon the muscles of the lips. Then after persisting for a long time with the movements of the fleshy part of the organ of speech, namely the tongue, we submitted it also to the same exercises, but varied them much more and continued them for a longer time.

XLI. Prepared in this way, it seemed to me that the organ of speech ought to lend itself without further trouble to the imitation of articulate sounds and I considered this result both near and inevitable. I was entirely mistaken. This long preparation resulted in nothing but the emission of unformed monosyllables sometimes shrill, sometimes deep and still far less clear than those which I had obtained in my first experiments. Nevertheless, I persisted, and still struggled for a long time against the obstinacy of the organ. Finally, however, seeing that the continuation of my efforts and the passing of time brought about no change, I resigned myself to the necessity of giving up any attempt to produce speech, and abandoned my pupil to incurable dumbness.

Third Series:

DEVELOPMENT OF EMOTIONAL FACULTIES

XLII. My Lord, you have seen civilization arousing the intellectual faculties of our savage from their complete torpor, first by fixating his needs upon the objects in his environment, and secondly by extending the range of his ideas beyond his animal existence. In the same order of development your Excellency will see the emotional faculties first awakened by the feeling of need arising from the instinct of self-preservation, then giving birth to less selfish feelings, to more expansive impulses, and to some of those generous feelings which are the glory and happiness of the human heart.

XLIII. On his entrance into human society Victor was quite insensible to all the care that was immediately taken of him. He did not distinguish between the eagerness of curiosity and the interest of good will, and for a long time there was no evidence that he paid any attention whatever to the person who looked after him. Approaching her when forced by need, or going away when satisfied, he saw in her only the hand which fed him and in that hand nothing but what it held. From the moral point of view, Victor was like a child in the earliest days of life passing from its mother's breast to its nurse's, and from hers to another's without discovering any difference other than that of the quantity or quality of the fluid which served for food. When taken out of his forest, it was with the same indifference that our savage saw the people, to whose care he was committed, changed at various intervals. After being welcomed, cared for and conducted to Paris by a poor peasant of *Aveyron* who lavished upon him all the tokens of a father's love, he underwent sudden separation from his benefactor without reluctance or regret.

XLIV. During the first three months after his entrance into the Institution he was left to the importunities of the curious idlers of the capital and to those who, under the special title of observers, gave him just as much trouble. He was left to wander in the corridor and garden of the house in the severest weather of the year, to crouch in disgusting filth and often to experience hunger. Yet, when he suddenly found himself cared for, cherished and caressed by a kind and intelligent guardian of gentle disposition, the change did not appear to awaken in him the slightest feeling of gratitude. But after a little reflection this does not seem surprising. As a matter of fact, what influence could be exerted by the most caressing ways or the most affectionate care upon so impassive a being as this! And what could it matter to him that he was well clothed, well warmed, comfortably lodged, and able to sleep on a soft bed—a creature who, hardened to the inclemency of the seasons, insensible to the advantages of social life, knew no happiness other than liberty and saw in the most comfortable lodging only a prison! In order to arouse gratitude, there were needed benefits of a different kind, such as could be appreciated by the extraordinary creature who was their object. Thus it would be necessary to comply with his tastes and make him happy in his own way. I devoted myself to this idea, regarding it as the principal factor in the moral education of this child. I have already related my first success in this direction.

In my original report I have told how I induced him to love his governess, and how I made social life bearable for him. But this affection, tender though it appeared, might still be considered as nothing but a calculation of self-interest. I had reason to suspect this when I noticed that after several hours and even after some days, although Victor returned to his guardian with demonstrations of affection, these expressions of delight were proportionate not so much to the length of his absence as to the real advantages which he found on his return and to the privations which he had experienced during this separation. His caresses were no less self-interested. He employed them at first to express his desire rather than his gratitude, and if he was carefully watched at the end of a copious meal, he presented the distressing spectacle of a creature who, from the moment when his needs were satisfied, was no longer interested in anything about him. However, as the ever increasing number of his desires rendered his connections with us and our cares for him more and more numerous, his obdurate heart at last opened to unequivocal feelings of gratitude and affection. Among numerous incidents that I could cite as so many proofs of this favorable change, I shall content myself with reporting the two following.

XLV. The last time when his memories and his passion for the freedom of the fields, led our savage to escape from the house, he turned in the direction of Senlis and gained the forest. He soon came out, however, doubtless driven by hunger and the impossibility of providing for himself any longer. Drawing near to the neighboring fields, he fell into the hands of the police who arrested him as a vagabond and kept him as such for a fortnight. Recognized at the end of this time and again brought to Paris, he was taken to the Temple, where Madame Guérin, his guardian, came to claim him. A number of inquisitive people had assembled to witness this interview, which was truly affecting. Scarcely had Victor caught sight of his governess, when he turned pale and lost consciousness for a moment but, as he felt himself embraced and fondled by Madame Guérin, he suddenly revived and showed his delight by sharp cries, convulsive clenching of his hands and a radiant expression. In the eyes of all the assistants he appeared less like a fugitive obliged to return to the supervision of his keeper, than like an affectionate son who, of his own free will, comes and throws himself in the arms of the one who has given him life.

XLVI. He was equally affected at his first interview with me. This was the following morning. Victor was still in bed. As soon as he saw me appear he sat up quickly, putting his head forward and holding his arms out to me. But seeing that, instead of coming near, I remained standing motionless in front of him and maintained a cold and displeased expression, he dived into bed again, covered himself with the bed clothes and began to cry. I increased his emotion by my reproaches, spoken in a loud and threatening tone. The tears redoubled and were accompanied by long, deep sobs. When I had carried the excitement of his emotions as far as possible, I went and sat on the bed of my poor penitent. This was always the signal of forgiveness. Victor understood me, made the first advances towards reconciliation, and all was forgotten.

XLVII. At about the same time, Madame Guérin's husband fell ill and was nursed away from the house without Victor being told of it. Having among his little domestic duties that of setting the table at dinner time, he continued to lay a place for Monsieur Guérin, and although he was made to remove it every day he never failed to set it again the next day. The illness had a sad end. Monsieur Guérin succumbed, and on the day when he died his place was again laid for him. One can guess what an effect such a distressing attention had upon Madame Guérin. Witnessing this scene of grief, Victor understood that he was the cause of it; and, whether he only thought that he had done wrong, or whether he penetrated the real reason of his governess's despair and felt how useless and misplaced were the pains he had been taking, he removed the place of his own accord, sadly put the things back in the cupboard, and never again set them.

XLVIII. Here was a sad emotion, belonging exclusively to the sphere of civilized man. Equally so is the profound state of moroseness into which my young pupil always falls when, in the course of our lessons, after struggling in vain with the whole power of his attention against some new difficulty, he realizes the impossibility of overcoming it. It is on such occasions, imbued with the feeling of his impotence and touched perhaps by the uselessness of my efforts, that I have seen him moisten with his tears the characters which are so unintelligible to him, although he has not been provoked by any word of reproach, threat or punishment.

XLIX. While multiplying his feelings of sadness, civilization ought to have increased his pleasures also. I will not speak of the pleasures born of the satisfaction of his new needs. Although they have contributed powerfully to the development of his emotional faculties, they are, if I may thus express it, so animal that they cannot be admitted as direct proofs of the sensibility of his feelings. But I will cite such evidences as the zeal which he employs, and the pleasure which he derives, in helping the people of whom he is fond, even in anticipating their wishes by little services which it is within his ability to render. This is to be noticed above all in his relations with Madame Guérin. I will also attribute to the feeling of a civilized being the satisfaction which spreads over his whole face and which often even finds expression in great bursts of laughter when, after being held up in our lessons by some difficulty, he finally succeeds in surmounting it by his own efforts; or when I am pleased

with some slight progress and show my satisfaction by com-
mendation and encouragement. It is not only in his exercises
that there is evidence of his pleasure in doing well, but also
in the most trivial domestic occupations with which he is
entrusted, especially if these occupations are of a nature to
require great development of muscular strength. For example, when he is employed in sawing wood he may be seen
to redouble his eagerness and his efforts, in proportion as
the saw cuts more deeply. On these occasions at the moment
when the wood is about to divide, he indulges in extraordinary expressions of delight that would tempt one to report
him as a raving maniac were there not a natural explanation. I refer to the need of movement in so active a creature,
and the nature of this occupation which, in presenting him
simultaneously with a salutary exercise, a mechanical activity which amuses him, and a result which touches his
needs, thereby offers him an unmistakable combination of
pleasure and utility.

L. But at the same time as the soul of our savage opens
up to certain enjoyments of civilized man, it continues no
less to prove itself sensitive to those of his primitive life.
There is always the same passion for the country, the same
ecstasy at the sight of a beautiful bright moon or a field
covered with snow, and the same transports at the noise of
a stormy wind. His passion for the freedom of the open
fields is certainly tempered by his social affections and half
satisfied by frequent walks out of doors; but it is a passion
still only half extinguished, and all that is necessary to re-
kindle it is a beautiful summer evening, the sight of a
deeply shaded wood, or the momentary interruption of his
daily walks. Such was the cause of his last flight. Madame
Guérin was kept to her bed by rheumatic pains and could
not take her pupil out during the fortnight of her illness.
Evidently understanding the cause of this privation, he bore

it patiently. But as soon as his governess left her sick bed, his happiness burst forth, and became still greater when, on a very beautiful day, he saw her prepare to go out. No doubt she is going for a walk, and here he is all ready to follow his guide! She went out and did not take him. He concealed his disappointment, but when at dinner time he was sent to the kitchen for the dishes, at the moment when the carriage gate in the court happened to be open to let a carriage through, he seized the opportunity of slipping behind it and, hurrying into the street, rapidly gained the *Barrière d'Enfer*.[22]

LI. The changes wrought by civilization in the young man's soul have not been limited to the awakening of affections and unknown pleasures; they have also brought to light some of those feelings which constitute what has been called righteousness. Such is the inner sense of justice. On leaving his forests, our savage was so little susceptible to this sense that for a long time it was necessary to watch him carefully in order to prevent him from indulging his insatiable rapacity. It may easily be guessed, however, that as he experienced at this time only a single need, namely, that of hunger, his thefts were confined to the few foods which were to his taste. In the beginning he took rather than stole them; and it was with a naturalness, an ease, a simplicity which had something touching about it and brought back to mind the dream of those primitive times when the idea of property was yet to dawn in the human mind. In order to repress this natural propensity towards thieving, I made use of chastisements applied during the very act. I reaped what society generally does reap from terror of its corporal punishments, namely a modification of the vice rather than a real correction of it. Victor stole with cunning what until then he had been content to steal openly.

[22] One of the outer gates of Paris (tr.).

I believed that I ought to try some other means of correction, and in order to make him feel more intensely the impropriety of his thefts we resorted to the law of retaliation. Thus on one occasion he was made a victim of this most powerful law by having a long-coveted fruit—one which had often been the just reward of his docility—taken out of his hands and eaten before his eyes; at other times, robbed by cunning rather than violence, he found his pockets emptied of the little provisions which he had put in reserve an instant before.

LII. These last methods of repression had the success which I had expected of them and put an end to the greediness of my pupil. This correction in conduct, however, did not appear to my mind to be a certain proof that I had inspired my pupil with the inner sense of justice. In spite of the care that I had taken to give to our proceeding all the forms of an unjust and obvious theft, I felt it was not certain that Victor had seen in them anything more than punishment of his own misdeeds. Consequently his conduct was due to the fear of new privations, rather than to disinterested moral motives. In order to clear up this doubt and to obtain a less ambiguous result, I thought I ought to test my pupil's moral reactions by submitting him to another species of injustice, which, because it had no connection with the nature of the fault, did not appear to merit punishment and was consequently as odious as it was revolting. I chose for this really painful experience a day when after keeping Victor occupied for over two hours with our instructional procedure I was satisfied both with his obedience and his intelligence, and had only praises and rewards to lavish upon him. He doubtless expected them, to judge from the air of pleasure which spread over his whole face and bodily attitude. But what was his astonishment, instead of receiving the accustomed rewards, instead of the treatment which

he had so much right to expect and which he never received
without the liveliest demonstrations of joy, to see me suddenly assume a severe and menacing expression, rub out
with all the outward signs of displeasure what I had just
praised and applauded, scatter his books and cards into all
corners of the room and finally seize him by the arm and
drag him violently towards a dark closet which had sometimes been used as his prison at the beginning of his stay
in Paris. He allowed himself to be taken along quietly until
he almost reached the threshold of the door. There suddenly
abandoning his usual attitude of obedience he arched himself
by his feet and hands against the door posts, and set up a
most vigorous resistance against me, which delighted me so
much the more because it was entirely new to him, and
because, always ready to submit to a similar punishment
when it was merited, he had never before, by the slightest
hesitation, refused for a single moment to submit. I in-
sisted, nevertheless, in order to see how far he would carry
his resistance, and using all my force I tried to lift him
from the ground in order to drag him into the room. This
last attempt excited all his fury. Outraged with indignation
and red with anger, he struggled in my arms with a violence
which for some moments rendered my efforts fruitless; but
finally, feeling himself giving way to the power of might,
he fell back upon the last resource of the weak, and flew at
my hand, leaving there the deep trace of his teeth. It would
have been sweet to me at that moment could I have spoken
to my pupil to make him understand how the pain of his
bite filled my heart with satisfaction and made amends for
all my labor. How could I be other than delighted? It was a
very legitimate act of vengeance; it was an incontestable
proof that the feeling of justice and injustice, that eternal
basis of the social order, was no longer foreign to the heart
of my pupil. In giving him this feeling, or rather in provok-

ing its development, I had succeeded in raising primitive man to the full stature of moral man by means of the most pronounced of his characteristics and the most noble of his attributes.

LIII. In speaking of the intellectual faculties of our savage I have not concealed the obstacles which arrested the development of certain of them, and I have made it my duty to describe exactly the gaps in his intelligence. Following the same plan in my account of this young man's emotions, I will disclose the animal side of his nature with the same fidelity as I have described the civilized side. I will suppress nothing. Although he has become sensible to gratitude and friendship, although he appears to feel keenly the pleasure of usefulness, Victor remains essentially selfish. Full of alacrity and cordiality when the services required of him are found to be not opposed to his desires, he is a stranger to that courtesy which measures neither privation nor sacrifice; and the sweet sentiment of pity is yet to be born within him. If in his relations with his governess he has sometimes been seen to share her sadness, this is only an act of imitation, analogous to that which draws tears from a young child who sees his mother or nurse weep. In order to commiserate with other people's troubles, it is necessary to have known them, or at least be able to imagine them. This cannot be expected from a young child or from such a creature as Victor, foreign as all those pains and privations which are the basis of our emotional sufferings are to him.

LIV. But what appears still more astonishing in the emotional system of this young man, and beyond all explanation, is his indifference to women in the midst of the violent physical changes attendant upon a very pronounced puberty. Looking forward to this period as a source of new sensations for my pupil and of interesting observations for myself, watching carefully all phenomena that were forerunners of this mental crisis, I waited each day until some breath of that universal sentiment which moves all creatures and causes them to multiply should come and animate Victor and enlarge his mental life. I have seen this eagerly awaited puberty arrive or rather burst forth, and our young savage consumed by desires of an extreme violence and of a startling constancy and this without any presentiment of its purpose or the slightest feeling of preference for any woman. Instead of that expansive impulse which precipitates one sex towards the other, I have observed in him only a sort of blind and slightly pronounced instinct which, as a matter of fact, does make him prefer the society of women to that of men without in any way involving his heart. Thus I have seen him in a company of women attempting to relieve his uneasiness by sitting beside one of them and gently taking hold of her hand, her arms and her knees until, feeling his restless desires increased instead of calmed by these odd caresses, and seeing no relief from his painful emotions in sight, he suddenly changed his attitude and petulantly pushed away the woman whom he had sought with a kind of eagerness. Then he addressed himself without interruption to another woman with whom he behaved in the same way. One day, nevertheless, he became a little more enterprising. After first employing the same caresses, he took the lady by her hands and drew her, without violence however, into the depths of an alcove. There, very much out of countenance, and showing in his manners and in his extraordinary facial expression an indescribable mixture of gaiety and sadness, of boldness and uncertainty, he several times solicited the lady's caresses by offering her his cheeks, and walked slowly round her with a meditative air, finally flinging his arms about her shoulders and holding her closely by the neck. This was all, and these amorous demonstrations ended, as did all the others, with a movement of annoyance which made him repulse the object of his transitory inclinations.

LV. Since this time although the unhappy young man has been no less tormented by this natural ebullition, nevertheless he no longer seeks to relieve his restless desires by fruitless caresses. But instead of alleviating his situation this resignation has served only to exasperate him and has led the unfortunate creature to find nothing but a cause for despair in an imperious need which he has given up hope of satisfying. When this storm of the senses breaks forth anew in spite of the help of baths, of a soothing diet and violent exercise, there follows a complete change in the naturally sweet character of this young man. Passing suddenly from sadness to anxiety, and from anxiety to fury, he takes a dislike to all his keenest enjoyments; he sighs, sheds tears, utters shrill cries, tears his clothes and sometimes goes as far as to scratch or bite his governess. But even when he yields to a blind fury which he is not able to overcome, he gives evidence of a real repentance and asks to kiss the arm or hand which he has just bitten. In this state his pulse is raised and his face apoplectic. Sometimes blood flows from his nose and ears. This puts an end to the transport, and further postpones a recurrence of the outburst, especially if the hemorrhage is abundant. Starting from this observation I have been obliged, in order to remedy this state and because I could not or dared not do better, to attempt the use of bleeding, not, however, without many misgivings because I am persuaded that true education should cool and not extinguish this vital ebullition. But I ought to say that if I have obtained a measure of calm by this means and many others which it would be quite useless to enumerate here, this effect has only been transitory; and the result of this continual desire, as violent as it is indeterminate, has been an habitual state of restlessness and suffering which has continually impeded the progress of this laborious education.

LVI. Such has been the critical period which promised so much and which would, without doubt, have fulfilled all the hopes which we had entertained for it, if, instead of concentrating all its activity upon the senses it had also animated the moral system with the same fire and carried the torch of love into this benumbed heart. Nevertheless, on serious reflection, I will not conceal the fact that when I counted on this mode of development of the phenomena of puberty, I was not justified in comparing my pupil, mentally, to an ordinary adolescent in whom the love of women very often precedes, or, at least always accompanies the excitement of the reproductive organs. This agreement between need and inclination could not occur in a creature whose education had not taught him to distinguish between a man and a woman, and who was indebted solely to the promptings of instinct for his glimpse of this difference without being able to apply it to his present situation. Also I did not doubt that if I had dared to reveal to this young man the secret of his restlessness and the aim of his desires, an incalculable benefit would have accrued. But, on the other hand, suppose I had been permitted to try such an experiment, would I not have been afraid to make known to our savage a need which he would have sought to satisfy as publicly as his other wants and which would have led him to acts of revolting indecency. Intimidated by the possibility of such a result, I was obliged to restrain myself and once more to see with resignation these hopes, like so many others, vanish before an unforeseen obstacle.

Such, my Lord, is the record of the changes that have taken place in the emotional system of the *Savage of Aveyron*. This section necessarily exhausts all the facts bearing upon the development of my pupil during the space of four years. A great number of them tell in favor of his capacity for improvement while others seem to indicate the opposite. I have made it my duty to present them all without distinction, and to relate my reverses as scrupulously as my successes. Such an astonishing variety of results adds an element of uncertainty to any opinion which can be formed of this young man, while the conclusions that can be drawn from the facts related in this memoir consequently present a certain lack of harmony.

Thus, bringing together those facts which are scattered through Sections VI, VII, VIII, XX, XLI, LIII and LIV, one cannot help concluding: first, that by reason of the almost complete apathy of the organs of hearing and speech, the education of this young man is still incomplete and must always remain so; secondly, that by reason of their long inaction the intellectual faculties are developing slowly and painfully, and that this development, which in children growing up in civilized surroundings is the natural fruit of time and circumstances, is here the slow and laborious result of a very active education in which the most powerful methods are used to obtain most insignificant results; thirdly, that the emotional faculties, equally slow in emerging from their long torpor, are subordinated to an utter selfishness and that his puberty, which was very strongly marked and which usually sets up a great emotional expansion, seems only to prove that if there exists in human beings a relation between the needs of the senses and the affections of the heart, this sympathetic agreement is, like the majority of great and generous emotions, the happy fruit of education.

But if the happy changes occurring in the state of this young man are recapitulated and particularly those related in Sections IX, X, XI, XII, XIV, XXI, XXV, XXVIII, XXX, XXXI, XXXII, XXXIII, XXXIV, XXXV,

XXXVII, XXXVIII, XLIV, XLV, XLVI, XLVII and XLIX, one cannot fail to consider his education in a more favorable light. The following conclusions are then perfectly justifiable. First, that the improvement of his sight and touch and the new gratification of his sense of taste have, by multiplying the sensations and ideas of our savage, contributed powerfully to the development of his intellectual faculties; secondly, when one considers the full extent of this development, among other real improvements he will be found to have both a knowledge of the conventional value of the symbols of thought and the power of applying it by naming objects, their qualities, and their actions. This has led to an extension of the pupil's relations with the people around him, to the faculty of expressing his wants to them, of receiving orders from them, and of effecting a free and continual exchange of thoughts; thirdly, that in spite of his immoderate taste for the freedom of open country and his indifference to most of the pleasures of social life, Victor shows himself sensible of the care taken of him, susceptible to fondling and affection, alive to the pleasure of well-doing, ashamed of his mistakes, and repentant of his outbursts; fourthly and finally, my Lord, looking at this long experiment from any point of view, whether it be considered as the methodical education of a savage or as no more than the physical and moral treatment of one of those creatures ill-favored of nature, rejected by society and abandoned by medicine, the care that has been taken and ought still to be taken of him, the changes that have taken place and those which can be hoped for, the voice of humanity, the interest inspired by such a complete desertion and a destiny so strange—all these things recommend this extraordinary young man to the attention of scientists, to the solicitude of our administrators, and to the protection of the Government.

INDEX